W

Wisdom. Wonder. Woman.

A 90 DAY ACTIVATIONAL

Preface

This little book is far more than just a daily devotional—it is what I call an "Activational." It is like a devotional . . . but more. Each day offers fresh revelation on critical matters of the heart, followed by a prayer impartation and personal activation.

Every power-packed page is filled with insight and wisdom intended to transform and mobilize women into their divine and powerful identity and purpose as they go out into the world, empowered by the Spirit.

Though written for women, this Activational is applicable for everyone who desires empowerment for life and ministry.

Introduction

When I was a young girl, I did not know I was powerful. I did not know I had the power to change my life, my relationships, my world, and the world around me. I thought I had to live with a broken heart, broken relationships, and a broken world.

But then I met Jesus and His Holy Spirit.

He changed my mind. He changed my world. And He filled me with the power of the Holy Spirit to bring change everywhere He sends me.

He gave me the gift of prophecy. He has given it to you, too. Prophecy is hearing God's voice and speaking His words. Prophecy is the power of the Holy Spirit through the spoken and declared word of the Lord that can change your life, change your relationships, and change the world!

You see, words are powerful. Proverbs tells us life and death are in our words (Proverbs 18:21). Whatever comes out of our mouths affects everything around us—with life or death. When Jesus spoke to a fig tree and told it to shrivel up, *it did*! Yet, when He spoke to the widow's son who had died, he came back to life.

Everywhere I go, all around the world, I talk to women who are hungry for more. They want to see God move in and through their lives. They want to participate in the kingdom of God and bring heaven to earth. This is no surprise. God is bringing revival to the nations. There is a revival move of God coming, and within that move is another move—a move of God among women.

He is raising up a great company of women in our day! Psalm 68:11 declares, "The Lord gives the command; the women who proclaim the good tidings are a great host . . ." (NASB, emphasis mine). In the Hebrew, this verse is saying the King and Commander utters His voice and an army of women preach and demonstrate the good news (gospel). We are those women, armed with the word of God that *never* returns void, but always accomplishes what it is sent out to do (Isaiah 55:11)!

It is time we take our power back from the enemy, in word and deed, and fight for the *more*! How do we do that? We say what God says. We prophetically declare God's word, God's heart, and God's dreams over ourselves, our loved ones, our churches, our cities, and our nations!

I'm telling you that I'm telling you *that I'm telling you*—which means I'm prophesying over you right now—we were born for this. The devil has waged war against us since the beginning because of who we were created to be: a great, powerful, prophetic, company of world-changing, history-making, heart-restoring WOMEN!

As you begin this 90-day journey, expect to be changed.

Throughout these pages, you will learn how to take back your power and authority. You will begin to look at the circumstances around you with new eyes and perspective—from heaven to earth. You will prophesy to the mountains in your life and see them removed. You will become a woman who knows her God, stands with the sword of the Spirit in her hands and the word of the Lord in her mouth, and causes the enemy to tremble.

Let's pray.

Father, in the mighty, unmatched name of Jesus, Your Word says that where two or three agree, whatever we ask for in Your name we receive. Therefore, Father, we agree that there is more, and so we ask that You raise us up in the knowledge of Your Word, in the power of the Spirit, in intimacy with You, and in our true identity as a great army who prophetically and supernaturally proclaims and demonstrates the good news of the kingdom—not only for ourselves, but for the ones we love and for every place and every person to whom You will send us. We want to see miracles! We want to see You move in our hearts, in our bodies, in our families, in our finances, in our government, and in our world! Now Lord, bless Your women and bring forth revelation and power for every breakthrough we need.

In Jesus' name,

Amen!

DAY 1: MY STORY

Knowing Jesus has made all the difference in my life.

Maybe it will comfort you to know that I have struggled for my own sense of identity. I have questioned my adequacy, ability, and choices in moments of fear or despair. And maybe it will comfort you to know that even though from the outside our lives exude confidence and successful achievements, from within, we who are ahead of you still question whether we have what it takes—whether in the end it will be judged good enough, and if, in fact, it has been enough for those who have depended on us.

Sometimes it seems that to be a woman, especially a woman who has birthed children, is to be guilt-conscious. Most of us are far too sensitive to guilt, and many of us have taken the "guilt trip" too seriously. The guilt trip is like an ancient art or skill passed down through the generations —you know, like basket-weaving, or pottery. Though it doesn't come with a training manual, I am sure it has full-color brochures!

My grandmother introduced the guilt trip to my mother, she introduced it to me, and I, of course, felt a responsibility, however false, to faithfully pass it on to all my daughters. Just so you know, in short course I refused the job. So should you. Trust me, the road of false guilt offers the same scenery it always has—a defective mirror of the past only revealing things you have not done or cannot undo, and a future forever failed in advance.

I don't believe that. I don't believe that we can ever make a mistake so big there is no redemption. So, I have taken a different road, and as cliché as it sounds, I suppose it is the road less traveled, because it really has made all the difference. Though I have struggled for my own sense of identity and questioned my adequacy, ability, and even choices in moments of fear or despair, I have found a life full of color and texture and meaning. And I have found faith.

I think this is what makes me—and any of us—wise. Wisdom is more than common sense. In fact, it is not common at all, but sacred. It is a knowing that redemption is the way. It is the way we treat each other, and the way we hold our children. It is the way we respond to trial, and the way we rejoice in victory. It is the hope we carry that buoys our dreams beyond our frailties and failings. It comes by faith. When I believe, all guilt is removed so that love becomes my lot. This is redemption.

And so, as we begin this journey together, I want you to know up front: *I don't know everything—but I believe.* This is what I hope I can share and impart. This is what has changed my life. I have lived my life in faith —faith in Christ and His redeeming work that is ongoing in my life, effectively shaping and changing me to make me ready for the good future that has already begun. That is what I believe. Every day. I believe it for me, for my family, and for you.

But, I haven't always been this way.

Family Brokenness

I have experienced many of the hard things a lot of women have experienced. The devil tried very hard to take my life away from me and keep me from ever becoming who God created me to be—a powerful woman of God. I thank God every day for finding me and saving my life.

I was born into a family that believed in Jesus but only attended church on occasion. When I was three years old, my father left our family and divorced my mom for a younger woman. When I was six, I was molested by a neighbor. At the age of seventeen, I developed an eating disorder that lasted many years. When I was nineteen, I was "left at the altar"—I was about to get married and the young man decided to start a sexual relationship with another woman a few weeks before the day. I had a nervous breakdown because of that rejection. At the age of twenty-one, I became pregnant and married a young man who was not a Christian and was addicted to drugs and alcohol. At the age of twenty-four, I had two children and filed for divorce.

In the middle of that story, when I was thirteen, I got "saved." Some friends invited me to a revival meeting at the Baptist church in town. I can't remember what the preacher said, but I remember feeling grief-stricken over my sin and wanting this Jesus who would forgive me, cleanse me, and be my

Savior. So, with tears streaming down my face and snot flowing from my nose, I walked all the way to the front of the church from the upstairs balcony to kneel at the altar and find Jesus. It was powerful and real. But I did not yet walk by faith and follow Jesus.

The Voice and a Promise

It wasn't until I was twenty-four and in the middle of a nasty divorce that my life turned down a redemptive path. After living for nearly four years with a husband who would stay out all night, come home drunk, and curse me, I had moved out of the house with my girls and into my own apartment. I had a boyfriend, and my soon to be ex-husband had a girlfriend. I was depressed, ashamed, and very broken.

Three weeks before our divorce was final, I happened to meet a woman who was married to a pastor. They were planting a new church in the area where I lived. She liked me and invited me over to her house. Over coffee, I told her the whole, ugly story. She was very kind to me and invited me to their new church. When I showed up there, no one judged me. No one tried to tell me how I should be living my life if I was a good Christian. I was simply welcomed into the community. There was no special counseling, group prayer meetings, or books offered to me. They just simply accepted me among them.

I felt so dirty, so hard. I had been so committed to living for any kind of personal fulfillment and pleasure. Funny, but these never come on your own terms, separated from God and your true identity in Christ. I was a stranger to myself—but to these people, I was one of God's children. I know this woman, and probably many others, were praying for me, but that was never thrown in my face so I would know I needed prayer for being so screwed up. My heart began to soften, and the numbness and self-protective guard began to melt. I cannot express to you how important this small segment of life is in my story.

One Friday, I was sitting in my living room while the children slept in the next room, when I heard the voice of God. It was very loud, clear, and outside and inside of me.

"Go home, and I will take care of everything," were the words I heard Him speak.

I was completely unhinged. I shot up from my chair, wildly looking around the room and talking back. "Do You know what You are saying? Do You know what You are asking of me? That man is not changed! He is still doing all the things he used to do."

But I knew. I knew in that very moment I was being asked to choose between life on my terms and life on His, and my answer would seal my future. Rebellion or obedience—there was no third option. I had not known that the Lord could speak to me. In all my early years of Sunday school, I had never once been taught that God speaks. Now I was faced with the most monumental choice in my entire life.

I made my choice. I called my husband and asked him to dinner with the kids. He was shocked, but came. During dinner, we had an angelic visitation. A woman came up to our table out of nowhere and said, "You are the most beautiful family I have ever seen." We hadn't sat together as a family for more than six months. I knew it was supernatural. I knew it was God confirming His word to me. I moved home within three days. Three more weeks and the divorce would have been final. That year, 1985, we had our third child. It was a miracle of grace.

The Promise Fulfilled

I went back to church on a regular basis, praying and trusting that the Lord would keep His promise to take care of everything that was broken in our lives. Though our marriage was surviving, my husband was still bound by addiction to alcohol and drugs, and I was still bound by an eating disorder. I spent many nights weeping in anguished prayer for God to fulfill His promise to me.

In 1988, we bought a house in Moorpark, California. I was happy about the chance to set up a house of my own, but I was fearful living so far from the city in which my husband worked and partied. Would he come home after his shifts? Would I be left alone, isolated from familiar haunts and friends? Would God intervene and fulfill His promise soon?

The day we moved in to our new house, God sent me a sign of hope. My husband gathered us all on the front porch to pray for God's blessing on our house, our family, and our new lives. It was not his custom to pray with the family. He seemed uninterested in God or the church. He was not a believer, though he said he believed there was a God and a Jesus. Four years after I had received God's promise, on the night before Thanksgiving, my husband left for another night of drinking.

I wept violently most of the night that Thanksgiving Eve, until I could not cry one more tear. *Did the Lord not see? Did He not care? Maybe I hadn't heard Him. Maybe I was crazy.* Then the hardness returned. I was done. I had prayed and cried out for help over and over and over. It was over. I was not hurt or mad—I was numb. I would leave and not return.

The next morning, I was readying the children for Thanksgiving dinner knowing I would be facing yet another round of questions, disapproving looks, and silent accusations regarding the foolishness of returning to a life like this. I realized that if I decided to leave my husband again, I would now have three children to raise on my own, with little sympathy and support from my family. As I was leaving the house, my husband came through the door, his face ashen white. I was disgusted, but he stopped me, telling me that something had happened. that had caused him to know I was going to leave again. He then begged me for one last chance, saying, "Things will be different this time, I promise."

I had given him so many last chances, and didn't believe he had changed, but I did not leave. Within a few weeks, however, I knew something had indeed changed. We sat down to talk.

He tells the story like this. He was out drinking with his friends. He knew he was blowing it again, like so many times before, but thought, *To hell with it. The wife can be mad if she wants.* It was the alcohol talking. It was almost morning when he began to drive home. Suddenly, a presence filled the atmosphere and he knew Jesus was in the car with him. Jesus told him he was about to lose everything he cared about and this time he would not get it back.

My husband surrendered his life to Jesus that night and was immediately, miraculously, and completely delivered from his addictions right then and there. He completely stopped using drugs and alcohol.

Each year, he celebrates his deliverance from addiction in gratitude to Jesus who saved his life and his family. This November 2018, we will have been married for 38 years.

God is so good.

Receiving My Calling

My husband's transformation began a time of healing for me and my family and prepared the ground of my life for the next move of God. I did not know it was coming, but it had been coming from the beginning. I had been rescued from myself, reconciled in marriage, healed from childhood/young adulthood trauma, and my sweet, young family was healing, growing, and attending a Foursquare church regularly. We had so much to be thankful for! It was more than enough for me. I was content. I did not need more.

Someone at church heard how God intervened in my marriage and asked me to come to a women's retreat to give my "testimony." I had never been to a women's retreat. I had never given a testimony. In my mind, I was still a Baptist girl in a Foursquare church. I did not have a Pentecostal or Charismatic understanding of Scripture. But I did know God and I wanted to speak up about what He had done for me. He had healed me. I had experienced God's voice once and watched Him do miracles in my family.

After giving my testimony, a young woman came up to me and said, "Kim, the Lord asked me to come and pray for you to receive the baptism of the Holy Spirit. Is that okay with you?"

"You can try," I said.

She put her hands on me and said some words I can't remember. I felt hot and faint, my knees began to buckle, and suddenly I was sitting in a chair. I could not really hear or concentrate on what was being said to me—something about how I should expect the gift of tongues to come, and to let it come when I got it. I made my way back to my room knowing something had happened, but not feeling much by then. I went to bed.

In the morning as I showered before the session, I heard some strange syllables in my mind. I struggled with my Baptist theology. Was this the devil? I knelt on the shower floor and prayed, "Lord, You say whatever I do, do it heartily unto You. So if I am being a fool, then I will be a fool for Jesus and do it heartily unto You." I began to speak in tongues. The naked truth is that I felt like an idiot, but I liked it.

On the walk to the morning session, I noticed color everywhere. It was like someone had removed a film from my vision and now colors were bright and blinding. As I passed a garden, I thought about how God's people were like the flowers—all different colors, varieties, and fragrances, all in differing stages of bloom. I thought about how pestilence comes against them, yet God sends the rain and the sunshine.

I arrived for worship, and a few minutes after I arrived, a woman began to sing loudly in tongues. Everyone else stopped singing and we listened. Silence. Then the same woman began to sing in English. I froze and became afraid as, word for word, she sang the thoughts I had just experienced about the garden. How could that be?

We moved into a time of communion. Each woman was supposed to take communion herself with the Lord. This was new for me. I sat and prayed something simple like, "Thank You Jesus for giving me Your life. I give You mine."

Then I heard a voice. "Will you water My garden?"

I froze with fear again. I was flooded with a knowing, which I now know is revelation. I knew He was calling me to full-time ministry. I began to weep.

The voice came again: "See the blonde woman over there? Go and tell her what has happened."

I robotically went and, through sobs, told the woman what I had heard. She put one hand on me, loudly spoke in tongues, and I think she commanded a spirit of self-doubt and fear to go. To this day I can't really say what it was she addressed by name. I shook violently, sobbed uncontrollably, and ran to my room.

17

Once in my room, it was as though the floodgates had opened and I heard the voice in torrents of instruction. "Go get your Bible. Get a paper and a pen. Write down what I tell you. Go to Hebrews Chapter 10. Read verses 19-25, 35-39. These will be your life Scriptures—especially verse 35...."

For several hours, He spoke to me. He delivered me of insecurity, intimidation, false humility, and false responsibility. He told me in detail what to do for the next five years, as I was entering into a time of preparation. I had known nothing of the Holy Spirit. I had never read my Bible all the way through. I was a mom from Moorpark, a labor and delivery nurse married to a fireman who was going to retire and live life on vacation at fifty-five. Now all was changed. I was changed. I was a different woman.

It was March 22, 1994. I have never been the same.

Whatever You Need, He Can Do It

This is my story, and it isn't over yet. I have seen countless miracles of salvation, transformation, healing, and redemption. And they have convinced me that there is nothing our God cannot do for us, no matter where we are in our stories.

Maybe you are reading this and you need a miracle. He can do it.

Maybe you need God to heal your heart of emotional or physical trauma. He can do it.

Maybe you need God to heal and restore your marriage. He can do it.

Maybe you need God to deliver a loved one from addiction. He can do it.

Maybe you need God to change the direction of your life. He can do it.

Maybe you need God to bring you a friend who will not judge you but show you the love of Jesus. He can do it.

Maybe you need God to give you direction for your future. He can do it.

Maybe you need God to change the landscape of your life. He can do it.

He can do it, and He *will* do it.

That's why you are here right now. The Lord is here to meet you at your point of need and to change your life and the lives of those around you. In the pages to come, the Lord wants to teach you how to believe and pray for these things.

But right now, the first step is to acknowledge your need and invite Him in.

Prayer

Lord Jesus, I need You. I invite You into my life to show me how to live, heal the brokenness, cleanse me from sin, and change the course of my life. I want to encounter You, hear Your voice, and experience the love of God and the power of the Holy Spirit. I give You permission to do whatever You need to do to give me the life You want for me. In Jesus' name I pray, Amen.

DAY 2: THE KINDNESS OF GOD

"I have loved you with an everlasting love;
therefore I have continued my faithfulness to you.."
Jeremiah 31:3

"For God so loved the world, that he gave his
only Son, that whoever believes in him should
not perish but have eternal life. For God did not
send his Son into the world to condemn the
world, but in order that the world might be
saved through him."
John 3:16-17

If you have picked up this Activational I want you to know it is not an accident. Jesus is drawing you closer to change your life. He is the Author of life, and the life He offers is abundant—full of love, joy, peace, comfort, adventure, passion, and friendship like you have never known. He has given His life to rescue, redeem, and restore yours.

Not long ago, I had an experience I will never forget. I was in another country and had been sent to a very large church. That night, as I sat on the platform facing a nearly packed house, I was nervous. I had "heard things" about the pastor and the leadership, and had begun to build an offense. I saw the pastor doing some things that, in my opinion, were wrong, and it angered me.

Then, in the middle of worship, I had a visitation from the Spirit of God. I suddenly had a physical, spiritual, and mental revelation of the kindness of the Lord. He saw past the issues, the sin, the wrongs, the brokenness, and the religiosity—into their past and through to their future. *And He loved them.*

I fell to my knees and started weeping, right there in front of thousands of people. I couldn't get over it. I had judged them because I thought they were grieving God, but the heart of God was grieved over the toil and the suffering and the abuse they had suffered that drove them to this behavior. He was not

20

pointing to their sin; He was pointing at me and saying He wanted to touch them, heal them, minister to them, and give them a new day, a new season of relief from the heaviness and abuse of the past.

I was completely undone, right there on the platform. When it was time for me to minister, tears smeared my contact lenses so badly that I could barely see. I couldn't go to my notes. I just stood, weeping before them, telling them what the Lord was showing and saying to me. The pastor and the leaders began to weep. I ministered to each of them individually that night, before I ever preached and ministered to the people.

The point is this. The Lord is not looking at you to point out your faults or missteps. He is wanting to heal you. He is wanting to restore you. He is wanting to give you His love.

He is kind. He is *so very kind*. Do you want to know this kindness? Do you want to know the love of the God who created you and who looks past your faults, missteps, mistakes, and wrongdoings to the wounds and hardships that have driven you there? His name is Jesus. He has changed my life, and He will change yours, too. He will forgive and wipe away every sin, mistake, and regret from your past. He will give you a new life, a fresh start. He will transform you into the person you were born to be and empower you to fulfill the purpose for which you were created. He can do this because He is God's Son, who came into this world to die on a cross in our place, and when He did this, He made a way for us to be reconciled to God and rescued from Satan and death.

Perhaps you have never asked Jesus to come into your life to rescue, redeem, and restore you. Perhaps today you can see that He is drawing you, calling you, and reaching out to you.

Today is the day to respond.

Today is the day to give your life into His hands and let Him transform you with His lovingkindness.

Prayer

Father God, I want to know Your lovingkindness. I want to be healed and restored. I want to have a life that has meaning and purpose. I want to know who You created me to be. I want to live the life You dreamed for me and fulfill the purpose for which I was created. Right now, Father, I come to You and give my life into Your hands. I believe that Jesus is Your Son and He died for me. I ask You today to forgive me and heal me. Jesus, come into my life and be my Lord and Savior. Baptize me with Your Holy Spirit and empower me with His gifts and the power to hear God's voice and follow Jesus all the days of my life. Thank you, Lord! In the name of Jesus I pray, amen!

Welcome to the family of God! I am so proud of you!

Be sure to find a church family to love you and guide you in your new life.

DAY 3: THE PROMISE OF THE FATHER

And while staying with them he ordered them
not to depart from Jerusalem, but to wait for the
promise of the Father, which, he said, "you
heard from me; for John baptized with water,
but you will be baptized with the Holy Spirit not
many days from now."
Acts 1:4-5

"But you will receive power when the Holy
Spirit has come upon you, and you will be my
witnesses in Jerusalem and in all Judea and
Samaria, and to the end of the earth."
Acts 1:8

March 22, 1994. It is a date that I will never forget. It is the day I had an encounter with the Holy Spirit that changed my life. I was attending a women's retreat and a young woman approached me and said, "Kim, this may sound weird, but I feel like God is telling me to lay hands on you for the baptism of the Holy Spirit." When she laid hands on me and prayed, I had a radical encounter with the Spirit of God and have never been the same.

Growing up, I did not know there was anything more than salvation. I had never heard the message of receiving the Holy Spirit and power. The Book of Acts is clear. Jesus told His disciples about a promise of the Father that was coming. This promise was a baptism with the Holy Spirit and it would give them power for the mission ahead. They were to be His witnesses to the whole world, and apparently, they needed the Holy Spirit's power to do it.

Maybe you just gave your life to Jesus. Perhaps you have been a believer for years. Have you received the promise of the Father?

Prayer

Father God, Jesus told His disciples to wait for Your promise of the Holy Spirit. He told them that they would receive power when the Spirit came upon them. I want Your Holy Spirit, right now. In the name of Jesus, I ask You for the baptism with the Holy Spirit and power. Amen.

Activation

Invite the Holy Spirit to fill you and baptize you. Give Him permission to bring you His gifts and give you His power to be a witness for Jesus. You may feel your body get hot, tremble, or feel lightheaded. You may feel your legs become weak, or even begin to laugh or cry. You may hear strange syllables in your mind and begin to speak in a strange new language you do not understand. You may have a vision or speak in prophecy. It's okay. Relax and allow the Lord to be in control.

DAY 4: ONE IN NINETY CHALLENGE

Behold, now is the favorable time;
behold, now is the day of salvation.
2 Corinthians 6:2b

How beautiful upon the mountains are the feet
of him who brings good news, who publishes
peace, who brings good news of happiness,
who publishes salvation . . .
Isaiah 52:7

For "everyone who calls on the name of the
Lord will be saved." How then will they call on
him in whom they have not believed? And how
are they to believe in him of whom they have
never heard? And how are they to hear without
someone preaching?
Romans 10:13-14

You have a gift to give, your life is a message, and you have beautiful feet! Someone needs you to bring them the good news of salvation. Maybe you received salvation for the first time reading one of these devotions. Perhaps you have known Jesus as your Lord and Savior for years. Whether it has been hours or years, now is the day of salvation for someone who will come across your path in these ninety days.

God will bring them. All you have to do is to share your life and your story.

My daughter Molly befriended a young woman who had moved in down the street. After spending time together for weeks, one Sunday morning Molly invited her to church with us. I did not know the girl's family very well or if they had any relationship with God at all, but her parents gave her permission to come.

Nothing seemed unusual that Sunday morning. Church was good, but there were no fireworks. It was a sweet, simple service. On the way home, the young woman blurted out, "How can I have Jesus?" I was completely surprised. I had been so wrapped up in the Sunday morning routine that it hadn't even crossed my mind that perhaps this young woman was not saved and might want a relationship with Jesus! I pulled the car over on the side of the road and told her about this Jesus. When I asked if she wanted Jesus in her heart and to put her life in His hands, she shed tears as she said, "Yes."

There are people in your life right now who want to know, "How can I have Jesus?"

I want to challenge you to simply share what you know about Jesus to the one God highlights to you over the days we will spend together in this devotional time.

Now is day of salvation!

Prayer

> *Father, I want to be a messenger of good news for someone else. Bring someone across my path in the next ninety days who needs to know Jesus and receive salvation. In Jesus' name, Amen.*

Activation

Write out a short testimony of what you love most about having a relationship with Jesus on a notecard or piece of paper. Include a short story of the day you received salvation and how it changed your life. Read it over to yourself five times.

You are ready! Watch for your opportunity!

DAY 5: THE DAY OF PENTECOST

When the day of Pentecost arrived, they were all
together in one place. And suddenly there came
from heaven a sound like a mighty rushing
wind, and it filled the entire house where they
were sitting. And divided tongues as of fire
appeared to them and rested on each one of
them. And they were all filled with the Holy
Spirit and began to speak in other tongues as the
Spirit gave them utterance… And all were
amazed and perplexed, saying to one another,
"What does this mean?" But others mocking
said, "They are filled with new wine."
Acts 2:1-4, 12-13

But Peter . . . lifted up his voice and addressed
them . . . "For these people are not drunk . . .
But this is what was uttered through the prophet
Joel: 'And in the last days it shall be, God
declares, that I will pour out my Spirit on all
flesh, and your sons and your daughters shall
prophesy, and your young men shall see visions,
and your old men shall dream dreams; even on
my male servants and female servants in those
days I will pour out my Spirit,
and they shall prophesy.'"
Acts 2:14-18

Something strange and wonderful had happened. A sound. A sight. An
infilling. And then languages they had never spoken before poured out in
praise to God! What in the world was this? What did it mean? Peter explains.
"These are not drunk as you suppose," says Peter. "What you are seeing, and
what we are experiencing, is none other than the fulfillment of the prophecy
given us by the prophet Joel. The prophet Joel said the day would come when
the Holy Spirit would be poured out on all flesh and we would be empowered

to prophesy, and receive divine revelation from God Himself in the form of dreams and visions. *This is that!*"

The sights and sounds were the manifestation of the coming of the Spirit. It was an extraordinary divine visitation. The pouring out of the Holy Spirit created a new people of God—a people empowered, a people who were supernatural, a people distinct from every other people group because they were filled with God Himself. God's people would now be empowered to hear God's voice, speak in tongues they did not know, prophesy about the present and the future, and demonstrate the gospel with signs and wonders.

We are God's people.

Prayer

> *Father, I am Yours. I am one of Your people. I am a new creation because I am born again. I want to be empowered to be a supernatural new creation, filled with Your Holy Spirit. Fill me now with Your Spirit. Baptize me. Holy Spirit come and empower me. In Jesus' name, Amen.*

Activation

Invite the Holy Spirit to activate the gift of prophecy in your life. Ask Him to speak to you about His love for you. Remember, the Lord loves you. He will not condemn or speak harshly. He will speak of His love in ways that fill you with gladness. Listen, and write down what He speaks.

DAY 6: THE GIFT IS FOR US

"And as for me, this is my covenant with them,"
says the Lord: "My Spirit that is upon you, and
my words that I have put in your mouth, shall
not depart out of your mouth, or out of the
mouth of your offspring, or out of the mouth of
your children's offspring," says the Lord, "from
this time forth and forevermore."
Isaiah 59:21

And Peter said to them, "Repent and be baptized
every one of you in the name of Jesus Christ for
the forgiveness of your sins, and you will
receive the gift of the Holy Spirit. For the
promise is for you and for your children and for
all who are far off, everyone whom the Lord our
God calls to himself."
Acts 2:38-39

It doesn't matter where you live, how much money you make, what gender you are, or what generation you were born in. The Holy Spirit and all His gifts are available to you!

In Numbers 11:29, the prophet Moses releases a prophetic prayer saying all God's people will be like prophets who hear God's voice and experience prophetic speech and revelation. The prophet Joel declares in Joel 2:28 that the Spirit will be poured out, and it is a promise to everyone whom Jesus calls, irrespective of age, gender, or socio-economic persuasion. Isaiah confirms God's words will be put in our mouths and the promise is for all generations to come eternally. On the day of Pentecost, Peter declares, "For the promise is for you and for your children and for all who are far off, everyone whom the Lord our God calls to himself." In other words, not only the Jews, but also the Gentiles and people from every other nation on the earth can receive the gift of the Holy Spirit.

A friend of mine, Dr. Jon Ruthven, says, ". . . the major concern for Acts seems to be simply that people receive the Spirit."[1]

In other words, Jesus wants us all to be empowered with the Holy Spirit! He came and died so that we could be reconciled to the Father and receive the Holy Spirit. The Holy Spirit has been poured out from generation to generation forever. Repentance and water baptism open the way for receiving the promised Spirit. The promised Spirit is the Holy Spirit, the Spirit of prophecy. Prophetic speech, miracles, signs and wonders, healing, deliverance, and salvation are all a part of normal Christian life. They are signs of God working in the world.

Prayer

Father God, I believe Your Word. You have given Your Spirit to everyone, everywhere, no matter the time they live in. I want Your Holy Spirit. I want my mouth to be filled with Your words. I want to hear Your voice, speak Your words, and demonstrate Your love in powerful ways. Come Holy Spirit! I want more Lord! In Jesus' name, Amen.

Activation

Invite the Holy Spirit to give You His gifts. Invite Him to fill Your mouth with His encouraging words for everyone you meet today.

---

[1] Jon Mark Ruthven, *On the Cessation of the Charismata: The Protestant Polemic on Post-Biblical Miracles*, rev. ed. (Tulsa, OK: Word & Spirit Press, 2011), 251.

DAY 7: DECLARE THE TRUTH

"You will also decree a thing,
and it will be established for you;
And light will shine on your ways."
Job 22:28 (NASB)

The Hebrew word "decree" in this passage means a violent severing or division. What is being severed? Anything that keeps God's truth from being established so we walk in His light! We decree a thing by declaring God's Word. When we make a declaration, we are pronouncing a decision in a situation or circumstance in agreement with God's Word. God's Word is truth. We come into agreement with God, by His Word, so that His truth is established and all the power of darkness, sin, sickness, and Satan is severed from the situation. Light then shines on our way and we move forward.

Over the years, I personally have kept a notebook full of the Scriptures God has given to me to declare over myself and others. I have seen *big* changes as a result of decreeing His Word!

For example, if you are a fear
something like this:

> *Father God, in the name of Jesus, I declare I have not been*
> *given a spirit of fear! I am not afraid, anxious, intimidated, or*
> *fearful. Your love, right now, is casting out all my fear! I am*
> *powerful. I am loved. My mind is settled, at peace, and under*
> *the control of the Holy Spirit. My thoughts are calm, and my*
> *decisions are wise and sound. I am not confused, intimidated,*
> *or insecure in any way. I make good and wise decisions for*
> *myself and my family. I will be known as a powerful and*
> *confident person by all those around me. I have been*
> *empowered by the Holy Spirit to do whatever is in my hand to*
> *do. I am powerful because God is with me and in me by His*
> *Holy Spirit. I have the Father's love, feel the Father's love, am*

full of the Father's love and I love others the way I am loved.
Thank you, Jesus! Amen and Amen!

Activation

Ask the Holy Spirit to give you three Scriptures to declare over yourself or a situation you are in. Write out a personal prayer using them. Read the prayer out loud for several days in a row and thank God for establishing His truth in your life. Then watch your life change!

DAY 8: EASTER JOY

"The thief comes only to steal and kill and destroy.
I came that they may have life
and have it abundantly."
John 10:10

Today I would like to share with you a very personal letter I wrote to a young woman who asked me to tell her what I know about joy. My prayer for you is that you would replace her name with your own and read it as though it was written just for you, because it was. It is from my heart to yours.

Dear Jen,

Sunday is Easter. I went shopping yesterday to find an Easter dress and watched all the kids lined up to have pictures with the Easter Bunny at the mall. I had to laugh as they hopped up and down, clapping and squealing as he came out of his "house" to greet them. Most of them were all dressed up.

I remember when I was little getting all dressed up for Easter. Mom would buy me a frilly dress, white patent leather shoes, little, white, lace-trimmed socks, and of course, a white "pock-a-book" with white gloves. Oh, I thought I was so grown up— even now it brings a smile. The gloves and purse were my favorite pieces. There was just something about them that made me feel beautiful and elegant.

I kept the tradition going with my daughters. My daughter Nicole particularly liked the patent leather shoes and would wear them sock-less out to play for months afterwards. *Why not?* I thought. *It gives her joy.* I wanted her to have joyful memories, especially connected to Easter.

For many years, I was plagued with a memory that haunted me.

I must have been about six years old when it happened. I can still remember every detail. It was a beautiful Easter Sunday. It was sunny and warm, bursting with the glory of spring. New life was everywhere. My family had been to church, which was our Easter tradition, and then taken a trip to see the roses in bloom at The Gardens. Everyone was dressed in their Easter finery. My older brother was a in suit and tie, hair smoothed and combed to the side. My sister and I were in our dresses, hair curled and pulled back with barrettes, gloved hands clutching our purses with hidden chocolate treasures tucked inside. My dress was pink that year. I felt like a princess. I just knew I was beautiful and I was certain that everyone who was lucky enough to glance my way thought the same thing.

Dad had a new movie camera. He and Mom thought The Gardens the perfect spot to take family movies. Dad played director. Mom was set designer and in charge of props. We kids were lined up against the roses as backdrop. It was such a happy day. Dad yelled, "Roll 'em!" as we were instructed to "act natural" and "do something."

I am not sure what I was thinking, but I knew for sure that I was going to be the next famous actress. I began to walk up to the roses and tilt my head ever so slowly to dramatically smell each one. I was fantasizing and glorying in the fact that there was an audience to take in my incredible acting abilities. In reality, I was in my own little world, which I often was in those days. It is a place I can still go, I am somewhat embarrassed to admit.

Anyway, as the story goes, I was pretending and imagining all sorts of glorious things as time went by. At one point, I turned around to see the admiration on my parents' faces for all the astonishing drama I had given (and I was sure I had drawn a crowd by now) and found myself alone. My family had moved on. No one was there.

I did not know how long I had performed for an audience that was imaginary only, but suddenly in that moment I felt crushed. All that time I thought I had held the attention of those around me, especially my parents, when in reality, or so I interpreted, I was invisible and easy to walk away from. Of course, this was not the truth, but my little six-year-old heart shrunk and took my confidence with it. My mind embraced a critique that went something like this: *You're so stupid. How could you think that you were special? You're just a showoff and you look dumb. Your performances don't fool anybody. You're invisible because you're nothing special.*

From that moment on, each time I failed at something, made a mistake, or misspoke, the critic would whisper the message that began that day. Isn't it amazing how an event so simple can plant such a wicked seed whose roots entangle the heart and strangle the true identity of a person? Sounds a bit diabolical, doesn't it? I believe it is. I wonder how many of us hold back from being all we are created to be because of a whisperer who appeared one day after such an event.

Years passed and I became a woman. The memory of that day had faded and been buried by everyday life, but the critical whisperer was a permanent resident who did not respond to eviction notices, though I sent them regularly! As I said earlier, I felt haunted, and by that I guess what I mean is I could never just enjoy my life. I was always second-guessing, looking for approval, wondering if I was making a fool of myself. It was exhausting, really. But over time, because I had lived with it so long, I no longer recognized it as a problem. It had become . . . normal. I didn't know this wasn't the way it was supposed to be.

I know that now. I don't live like that anymore. I can't tell you the day it happened, where I was, or the time of day, but I know what I saw, the way I felt, and the change that took place inside of me.

I had children of my own. Life was good. I had begun to answer a call to ministry that had come unexpectedly and I was moving forward in adjusting my life to what I knew was being asked of me. It was exhilarating. My faith was deep and my relationship with Jesus deeper. It was during this time that I had an experience during prayer, which I would describe as a vision—a dream while awake.

I was conscious and coherent. I was not frightened. I suddenly was in a very spacious place that was white, simple, and quiet. I took a few steps forward and found myself standing before a large, throne-like chair with a large man sitting on it. He was dressed in white robes and he filled the chair and the room with his presence. I felt safe and comfortable. I could not see his face, for he was so great before me.

He gestured with his hands for me to climb up into his lap. I knew I wanted to. As I began the ascent, I suddenly caught a glimpse of myself. My arms and legs were small and childlike. On my feet were patent leather Mary Janes with white, lace-trimmed socks. When I finally was settled on the gentleman's lap, I looked down at myself and I was wearing a pink dress that was so familiar.

Somehow, I caught a glimpse of the scene from another vantage point up above. I was a little girl about six years old and I heard God, the Father, in whose lap I sat, say, in the most kind, loving, and gentle tone, "Now Kimmie, show me your pretty dress and shoes. I want to see. You are lovely to me."

The floodgate of emotion for all the years of torment and torture that had been released over me all those years before burst forth in torrents of tears. I felt a rending in my mind as the lie that I had believed was ripped out, roots and all. I felt my heart strain against its bindings until it broke free and expanded in fullness, lifting my confidence with it. The kindness of the words was a salve to my soul, healing me to the core.

I knew in that moment I was no longer captive to the lies of the whisperer. I would never believe those words again. I had been set free to enjoy my life, to love the mystery of myself, who God created, and to know that I have a Savior who cares about setting me free at every point of captivity and bondage that has restrained me from becoming what He has intended. I had been healed and set free to be who I truly am. And I am.

This is joy. This is Easter. Jesus comes to set the captives free and give them abundant life. He really saves.

Prayer

Father God, I want Easter joy. I want You to come and touch the deepest parts of me. Wherever the enemy has planted a lie inside my heart that has tormented me, show me the truth about what You think of me. I invite You to come into my life and save me, heal me, and be my Lord and Savior. Fill me with Your Holy Spirit and make me Your own. In Jesus' name, Amen.

Activation

Invite the Holy Spirit to bring to your mind the point in time when the enemy used a circumstance to plant a lie in your mind and heart. Then invite the Holy Spirit to come and give you a vision and encounter with the Lord that will break the power of the lie. Allow the Holy Spirit to fill you, deliver you, and implant the joy of the Lord in your heart afresh.

DAY 9: WOMEN ARE POWERFUL

The Lord gives the word;
the women who announce the
news are a great host
Psalm 68:11

"At strategic times in salvation history, God has
chosen women and empowered them with His
Spirit to carry out His will in extraordinary ways
. . . he called countless women and empowered
them to fulfill both humble and high-profile
assignments. In the 20th century, spirit-filled
women began to discover that these women
were not the exceptions to God's plan,
but instead were his prototypes for God's
woman."
Susan C. Hyatt[2]

Do you know you are powerful? Do you know you are anointed and appointed, called by God for this time we are living in? Do you know you have the power to change the world around you? Do you understand that knowing who you are, whose you are, and the power that is inside you makes you unstoppable, because the unstoppable God is with you, in you, beside you, and behind you?

Scripture and history both bear witness to the truth that women are powerful and have a part to play in God's plan for their own life and the lives of others. God is speaking and raising up an army to proclaim His Word—His powerful, revelatory, unstoppable good news.

---

[2]Susan C. Hyatt, Vinson Synan Ed., *The Century of the Holy Spirit: 100 Years of Pentecostal and CharismaticRewal, 1901-2001,* (Nashville, TN: Thomas Nelson, 2001) 262.

It's time! It is time to receive a fresh empowerment from the Holy Spirit. It is time to hear the voice of the Lord. It is time to awaken to who you really are. You can make a difference! All you need to do is open up to a fresh encounter with the living God right now!

Prayer

Holy Spirit, come. Fill me up! Empower me, stir up my gifts, and open my ears to hear and my eyes to see. Come and reveal to my mind and heart who God created me to be. Awaken me to my destiny! Come Holy Spirit! In the name of Jesus, for the glory of the living God, and by the power of the Spirit, change my perspective and give me a fresh vision from heaven! Amen!

Activation

Find a quiet place and time. Ask the Holy Spirit to give you a picture of who God created you to be. Draw the picture on a piece of paper. Then, ask the Holy Spirit to speak to you about what this picture reveals about your life, gifts, and divine purpose. Ask Him to give you a Scripture that applies to your life. Write it down and memorize it.

DAY 10: DIVINE APPOINTMENT

And He had to pass through Samaria . . .
John 4:4

Do not be conformed to this world,
but be transformed by the renewal of your mind,
that by testing you may discern what is the will of God,
what is good and acceptable and perfect.
Romans 12:2

John 4 records the incredible story of the woman at the well. She was a nameless, faceless woman with a questionable past and seemingly no future. Her life was marked by personal failure, cultural rejection, insignificance, isolation, and shame.

Jesus could have gone another way to Galilee, but Scripture says, "He had to pass through Samaria." Jesus didn't *have* to do anything. In fact, Jesus only did what the Father was doing. There was another route to His destination, but He "had to pass through Samaria" because *she* was there. He had a divine appointment to keep with a woman at a well. He had a plan for her life. Jesus came to redefine her past and release her into a new future. He knew her story and He wanted to bring to her a different ending.

Sometimes we miss the importance of this situation. Samaria was a culture mixed with what was considered unclean. Women, especially a woman from Samaria with such a questionable past, were considered insignificant if not unclean. According to Jewish religious leaders and the culture of the time, both Samaria and women of this nature were to be avoided.

Scripture is shouting to us. Jesus went to great lengths for this one woman. He went to the driest, hottest place. He crossed ethnic, cultural, gender, and religious boundaries to find her. He put Himself in danger to meet her. He even put His reputation on the line to capture her heart and call her to Himself.

She is all of us. He goes to great lengths and takes serious risks to reach us. He understands our frailty and brokenness. He meets us in our human condition, our doubts, our insecurities, our dryness, our loneliness, and our weakness.

> For we do not have a high priest who is unable to sympathize with our weaknesses, but one who in every respect has been tempted as we are, yet without sin. Let us then with confidence draw near to the throne of grace, that we may receive mercy and find grace to help in our time of need. (Hebrews 4:15-16)

Mercy is receiving what we do not deserve. Grace is the empowering presence of God. Jesus not only understands the suffering and sin of our lives, but also offers the power to transform it!

The truth is there is nothing in our past or present that can exclude us from being called into a glorious future with God in this hour because Jesus is our Savior, Redeemer, and Lord!

Prayer

> *Thank You, Jesus, for going to such great lengths to find me! Come and heal me, forgive me, and make me ready for the future. Give me a fresh understanding of who You are and how You love me. I no longer want to be conformed to this world's definition of who I am to be, so I ask You to come and renew my mind. I want to be the woman You see and whom You have called. In Jesus' name, Amen.*

Activation

Ask the Holy Spirit to reveal to you all the ways in which Jesus has gone to great lengths to reach you. Write them down. Think about what it means to you and how much He loves you to do such a thing. Take the time to thank Him for what He has done and worship Him for His goodness and kindness.

DAY 11: WELL MEANING

Jacob's well was there . . .
John 4:6

A defining moment is a moment when God comes and says, "You are not who you think you are! You are something more, and I have a plan. *My plan doesn't look like yours!*"

The Bible is full of defining moments. Moses and the burning bush. Gideon in the wine press. Isaiah and the vision of God on the throne. Jonah and the whale. Esther and the King. David and Goliath. Mary and the angel Gabriel. Paul on the road to Damascus. These all experienced a moment when God re-defined who they were and commissioned them into something new.

When the nameless, faceless woman at the well had her defining moment, it was in a very specific place—Jacob's well. It was a holy site pregnant with meaning. It was an allusion. An allusion in Scripture is how an author points to other events to enhance meaning. It is designed to bring to mind something from the past.

Wells are the place where bridegrooms find their brides. At a well, Abraham's servant found Rebekah (Genesis 24), Jacob found Rachel (Genesis 29), and Moses found Zipporah (Exodus 2). This particular well in John 4 was Jacob's well. Jacob is a patriarch or father of Israel. Jesus is part of the patriarchal tradition, and Hebrews says Jesus is, in fact, greater than Abraham, Isaac, Jacob, and even Moses. Just as these fathers, or patriarchs, found their bride at a well, so too, Jesus is seeking His Bride at Jacob's well. Just as these fathers, or patriarchs, found mothers, or matriarchs, at the well, so too does Jesus.

Jesus is surely seeking His Bride. But He is also just as clearly seeking mothers who will stand alongside fathers in this hour, matriarchs who will lead alongside patriarchs as co-heirs, co-kingdom bringers, co-leaders, and co-revivalists!

Jesus is looking for *you*. He is saying, "You are not who you think you are! You are something more and I have a plan. *My plan doesn't look like yours!*"

Prayer

> *Lord, bring me to a defining moment so that I can become all that You created me to be. I give You permission to change my life in whatever way You dream! In Jesus' name, Amen.*

Activation

Ask the Holy Spirit to reveal to you what it means to be a mother and a matriarch in the kingdom. How would this understanding change how you approach your work, your family, and your life?

DAY 12: CREATED FOR A PURPOSE

I praise you, for I am fearfully and wonderfully made.
Psalm 139:14

And we know that...all things work together
for the good of those called according to His purpose.
Romans 8:28

It is my life's pursuit to be a woman who lives by every word that proceeds from the mouth of God. Every year I take the time to sit before the Lord and ask Him four specific questions. It is my own personal strategy for being intentional about moving forward. Answering these questions encourages me to stay accountable to the revelation and empowerment God has given me. In the next several days, I will guide you through the questions and help you get a strategy for moving forward in the call on your own life.

But first, we need to talk about a few things.

Did you see the first *Captain America* movie? Captain America—Steve Rogers—is a weakling. He is small, sickly, and suffers opposition to his dreams for his life at every turn. One day, a man recognizes the good in him. This man sees that there is the heart of a lion in Steve Rogers and empowers him to become Captain America. However, even after he becomes able to fulfill his mission, those in leadership above him still see him as weak and foolish. He is forced to play a caricature of himself. He walks in a false identity, fulfilling a shadow mission where he is not living as his true self, using his true gifts. He is not fulfilling the purpose for which he was created and empowered. Captain America is discouraged and mad, but resigned to play the part they've given him. Until, that is, someone confronts him with the truth and says, "This is not what you were created for. What are you going to do about it?"

This is my question for you. How are you going to live your life differently because of the revelation you have received?

Are you ready to partner with God and do something about your life?

The following are comments I hear from a lot of people:

- ☐ My life feels out of control.
- ☐ I work so hard, but nothing seems to ever get done.
- ☐ I am busy all the time doing so many things, but I don't feel like I ever get to the things that are most important to me.
- ☐ You always seem to move forward.
- ☐ *How do you do that?*

When I first received the call of the Lord through a radical encounter with the Holy Spirit, it changed my entire life in a moment. I was having visions and dreams and receiving prophetic words everywhere I went from people I did not know. I had no idea what to do with them or how to walk them out.

At the time, I had my husband, three school-aged children, and a full-time job. There were times in my own walk when I simply *could not* lift the tiniest finger to participate in what God was doing in my life. I have experienced deep discouragement, bone-deep weariness, a health crisis, and intimidation so strong I felt immobilized for a time.

Sometimes we fall down, get sick, or become exhausted. In those times, we have to know that we know that we know God's love and grace are deeper than any pit into which we may fall. Corrie Ten Boom said that.

By God's grace, I managed to walk according to God's call on my life. *None of this can be accomplished in our own strength.* There are things that only God can do. Yet, we have a part to play, a responsibility as well. Jesus told a paralyzed man to take up his mat and walk. He had to actually *do* something. He had a part to play in walking out the call from Jesus.

Prayer

In your own words, make a fresh commitment to follow the Lord and obey His every word. Tell Him your fears and invite Him to change the way you see and think about your roles and relationships.

Activation

Get out your journal or a notebook and invite the Holy Spirit to be with you. Write about the roles you fulfill right now in your life, in your family, at your job, in your community, and at church. Are you doing what you were created for?

It is important before we even begin to ask the questions to decide and commit to acting on whatever He says. If the Lord asks you to change your roles, relationships, attitude, or anything else, are you willing to commit to change, even if it is hard?

DAY 13: FOUR QUESTIONS—
THE FIRST QUESTION

Therefore, my beloved, as you have always
obeyed, so now, not only as in my presence but
much more in my absence, work out your own
salvation with fear and trembling, for it is God
who works in you, both to will and to work for
his good pleasure.
Philippians 2:12-13

Draw near to God, and he will draw near to you.
James 4:8

God never asks us a question because He is looking to find out something He doesn't already know. He asks questions to bring us revelation of Himself, ourselves, and our circumstances. Revelation means information or understanding that has been hidden from us, but now is being revealed by God. His Word is revelation. It is light and life. It brings the light so that we can clearly see what is, what was, and what is to come. God does not want us to live our lives in the dark!

Each of the four questions has a specifically focused function. Each question is about what *God* wants to do. He is the center and the focus of our lives. If we want to live the life we were created to live, we must live to fulfill the desires of God's heart. In order to become who He created us to be, we must yield to *His* plan. We will have to give up our control and let Him be in control. We will need to align our heart and will with His and listen to what He wants to say.

Here is the first question: "What does God want to do *in* me?"

God is interested in us, personally. He is interested in our relationship with Him, and our growth and development as His child. We are His heart's desire! Asking this question allows God to speak to us about how He sees us, the ways in which He wants to be more intimate with us, and where He wants to bring personal growth and development into our lives.

Therefore, when we ask, "What does God want to do *in* me?" we are listening for the Holy Spirit's answers regarding what God wants to work on *inside of us* personally over the next year.

- ☐ Who does He say that we are?
- ☐ How does He see us, and how is that different from how we see ourselves?
- ☐ What kind of changes to our personal habits, attitudes, character issues, and belief systems does He want to make?
- ☐ What changes in our relationship with Him and in our relationship with ourselves does He want us to make?

Our God desires intimacy. He wants us to know we are loved. He wants us to know there is more for us than we are experiencing at present. He wants us to feel and experience His presence! Intimacy with God, through Jesus, by the power of the Holy Spirit, changes us from the inside out, opens our ears to hear His voice, and opens our eyes to see His face.

Intimacy with God always leads to identity. Our true identity is formed by God in intimate relationship with Him. The more intimacy we have with Him, the more we become who we truly are: beloved, complete, whole (holy), and powerful. We are worshippers in spirit and truth, empowered with all of Him within us. The more we become who God says we are, the more we increase in our ability to co-labor with Him! We can change the world!

Prayer

> *Father, I am so thankful to know that You care for me and desire to bring me close. You know my heart. I want to know Yours. I want to become everything You dreamed and created me to be. Speak to me, Lord. I am listening. In Jesus' name, Amen.*

Activation

Spend some time in a quiet place with a journal or notebook in hand. Invite the Holy Spirit to come. Ask the question, "What do You want to do *in* me this year, Lord? Listen for the answer and write it down.

DAY 14: FOUR QUESTIONS—
THE SECOND QUESTION

"Go into all the world and proclaim the gospel
to the whole creation . . . And these signs will
accompany those who believe:
in my name they will cast out demons; they will
speak in new tongues; they will pick up serpents
with their hands; and if they drink any deadly
poison, it will not hurt them; they will lay their
hands on the sick, and they will recover."
Mark 16:15-18

"You shall love the Lord your God with all your
heart and with all your soul and with all your
strength and with all your mind, and your
neighbor as yourself."
Luke 10:27

The second question is, "What does God want to do *through* me?"

Our salvation was only the beginning point of a journey in which we become the fulfillment of God-dreams and visions for all. God is interested in us coming to understand the purpose and call on our lives. In Matthew 28:28 and Mark 16:15-18, we discover the "go" of the gospel. The Great Commissions are for us all.

We are Jesus to the world around us! We are kingdom bringers! We are history makers!

Isaiah 61 and Luke 4:17-21 tell us the Spirit of the Lord was upon Christ, who was anointed to bring good news to the poor, bind up the brokenhearted, proclaim liberty to the captives, and open the prison doors for those who are bound. Christ is in us and now we are anointed to do the same. We all have a call to reach others, dispel the works of darkness, proclaim and demonstrate the gospel, and complete the mission of Christ on the earth until His return.

What we are called to do is clear. How we do it is particular to each of us individually.

Whether as an author, business leader, mother, nurse, teacher, evangelist, prophet, or something else entirely—in this next year what does God want to do through your life for others?

- ☐ Where will He send you?
- ☐ To whom and for what is He sending you?
- ☐ What is He desiring to accomplish in that place with those people for His purposes through you?

Prayer

> *Father, You are still asking, "Who will go for us?" Today, I am saying, "Here I am, Lord. Send me." Come and fill me again with Your Holy Spirit. Anoint me, guide me, and direct me. Give me marching orders! In Jesus' name, Amen!*

Activation

Spend some time in a quiet place with a journal or notebook in hand. Invite the Holy Spirit to come. Ask the question, "What do You want to do *through* me this year, Lord?" Listen for the answer and write it down.

DAY 15: FOUR QUESTIONS—
THE THIRD QUESTION

"No one can serve two masters, for either he
will hate the one and love the other, or he
will be devoted to the one and despise the
other. You cannot serve God and money."
Matthew 6:24

To illustrate the selected verse above from Matthew 6, N.T. Wright writes:

The student looked crestfallen, as well he might. For
weeks he had thought he was doing all right. Yes, he
hadn't been working as hard as he could have done; but
he was in the college football team, and he was playing
in a rock group, and he was reading some very exciting
novels . . . and somehow he hadn't been spending quite
as much time in the library as most of the others. Now
his tutor was facing him with the question. What were
his priorities? Did he want to get a university education
and degree, or did he just want to be at a wonderful
holiday camp? Of course, many students manage to
juggle dozens of different commitments and still end up
doing enough work to earn a degree. But frequently
they have to face difficult choices. You can't do
everything. What is really important? What will you
say, when you look back in ten years' time, 'I wish I'd
really given it my best shot'? or 'I'm glad I decided to
put all my effort into it'?[3]

The third question is, "What are the *priorities* God wants me to establish?"

---

[3]Tom Wright, *Matthew for Everyone, Part 1: Chapters 1-15* (London: Society for Promoting Christian Knowledge, 2004), 61–62.

Priorities are those things we determine to truly value. Priorities are the things we hold as sacred in our lives. What will we guard?

Priorities are the things to which we dedicate our resources, whether physical, emotional, intellectual, financial, or relational. Time is the most significant resource of all. We all have the same amount of time in a day, a month, or a year. How we spend our time makes all the difference. We all have significant relationships to protect and value. We all have one physical body to care for. We all have a limited capacity for emotional and financial expenditure.

For example, I am a full-time itinerant minister. I travel a *lot*. In order to be mentally, emotionally, and physically healthy, I must get enough sleep, exercise, good food, and play time with friends. In order to have a strong marriage and family life, I must make time with my husband and children a priority. In order to be an effective minister, I must have a fresh and intimate relationship with Jesus, and the time to read the Word and listen to the voice of the Lord. When I have intimacy with Jesus, am in good health, and have strong relationships, I am not only more effective in ministry, but I also create the potential for longevity. These are a few of my personal priorities. *Revival is coming! God is moving in extraordinary ways on the earth right now! It is His desire to strengthen every aspect of your life and release you further into the purposes for which you were created!*

And so, allow God to establish your priorities! Refuse to settle for anything less than everything God has for you!

Prayer

> *Father! I know that You have a plan for my life. I want to walk in Your plans! I want to fulfill Your dreams! I do not want to settle for what might be good when there is more. I want Your best for my life! I want to be ready for the revival You are bringing. Make me ready! In Jesus' name, Amen.*

Activation

Spend some time in a quiet place with a journal or notebook in hand. Invite the Holy Spirit to come. Ask the question, "What are the priorities You want me to establish this year?" Listen for the answer and write it down.

DAY 16: FOUR QUESTIONS—
THE FOURTH QUESTION

But Martha was distracted with much serving.
And she went up to him and said, "Lord, do you
not care that my sister has left me to serve
alone? Tell her then to help me." But the Lord
answered her, "Martha, Martha, you are anxious
and troubled about many things, but one thing is
necessary. Mary has chosen the good portion,
which will not be taken away from her."
Luke 10:40-42

Brothers, I do not consider that I have made it
my own. But one thing I do: forgetting what lies
behind and straining forward to what lies ahead,
I press on toward the goal for the prize of the
upward call of God in Christ Jesus.
Philippians 3:13–14

A river without banks is a flood. When water flows within banks on either side, we call it a stream or a river. A river is full of twists and turns but is always going in the same direction with a single purpose—to reach the sea!

Our lives are like a river. They are not meant to be purposeless or directionless like a flood. Our lives and personal resources are meant to flow in one direction, which is toward the fulfillment of God's will, promises, and dreams for our lives, all the while empowered by the Holy Spirit.

Like banks to a river, priorities and boundaries keep us strong, focused, and going on one direction—forward.

The fourth question is, "What are the *boundaries* God wants me to establish?"

We cannot keep our priorities if we have no boundaries!

Jesus had both priorities and boundaries. Jesus is 100% love, 100% merciful, 100% compassionate and He stayed 100% true to His identity and mission. Jesus is our model. He is fully man and fully God. He lived by the power of the Holy Spirit, hosting the presence of God at all times. He lived with powerful boundaries. Jesus repeatedly said He had to be about His Father's business first and foremost. He was moved with compassion by human need, but He was never pulled away from His first priority because of it.

- When His family called to Him to come out of the house where He was speaking, because they were afraid He was crazy, He said, "No."
- When Martha and Mary called for Him to come right away because Lazarus was sick and dying, He said, "No." He stayed where He was two more days and Lazarus died.
- When Peter tried to stop Him from going to the cross, Jesus told him, "No," and even said, "Get behind me, Satan!" (Matthew 16:23).
- When He came to the pool of Bethesda He said to the crippled man, "Do you want to be healed?" (John 5:6).

Priorities are the things we give our attention and resources to. Boundaries are the things we don't give them to. Boundaries help us discern what to say "No" to—things like distractions, the good but not best, unnecessary arguments, unproductive or abusive relationships, time-wasters (like computer games and TV), crisis that is not really crisis, or the enemy. Without boundaries, priorities become muddled and eventually disappear.

It is as important to say *"No"* and it is to say "Yes." *Learn to say "No!"* Establish boundaries.

Prayer

> *Father, You know my life. You know everything about me. You know all about the areas in my life where there are no "banks to the river" and it has become a flood and is unmanageable and unproductive. I want to move forward. I need Your wisdom! I am asking for Your wisdom, Lord, and for Your Holy Spirit to lead me now. In Jesus' name, Amen.*

Activation

Spend some time in a quiet place with a journal or notebook in hand. Invite the Holy Spirit to come. Ask the question, "What are the boundaries You want me to establish this year?" Listen for the answer and write it down.

DAY 17: NOT YOUR GRANDMOTHER'S ACCOUNTABILITY

Then the Lord God said,
"It is not good that the man should be alone;
I will make him a helper fit for him."
Genesis 2:18

Two are better than one, because they have a
good reward for their toil. For if they fall, one will
lift up his fellow. But woe to him who is alone
when he falls and has not another to lift him up!
Ecclesiastes 4:9-10

Before we leave our devotions with the four questions, let's talk about accountability.

We were created for intimacy. Intimacy cannot happen in isolation, because intimacy happens in relationship! Therefore, we were also created to be in community. It is within community we discover our true identity, grow, and fulfill the purpose for which we were created.

Accountability has been misunderstood. Somewhere along the line it became the vehicle for punishing those who failed to perform according to a rule of standard in the church. Accountability is actually about being held to account for stewarding the gifts and call of God on our lives. It is the vehicle by which we challenge and encourage one another to become who God desires us to be—calling each other up to the high calling of God.

There are two persons to whom we need to be accountable: God and ourselves.

Being accountable to ourselves is about personal integrity. I am the first person to be affected negatively by continuously making and breaking commitments, especially to myself. Maintaining integrity to commitments made to myself overflows into maintaining integrity in commitments I make to others. The more I honor my commitments to myself and the revelations God has given me, the more I grow in confidence in who God has created me to be.

Being accountable to God means submitting ourselves to the inspired, God-breathed, written Word (2 Timothy 3:16), the voice of God (John 10:27), and the community of faith (Hebrews 10:24-25). This means we walk by the Spirit of God. We allow Father, Son, and Holy Spirit to examine and align our hearts by the written Word. We listen for His voice and obey His Word. We make ourselves available to the community of faith for the sharpening and shaping of our lives within authentic relationships.

This is so important. In asking these four questions, we are asking the Spirit of the living God to speak to us. When He speaks, we are accountable for the commitments we make to the Lord and ourselves. Staying accountable and being obedient to what He says to us accelerates the growth and forward movement in our lives.

Now that we have answered all four questions, it is time to share them with those God has placed in our lives for accountability in this season, who He will reveal to us. It will release an acceleration!

Prayer

> *Father, You said it isn't good for me to be alone. You want to give me support and encouragement through community so that I can become everything You created me to be. Send me friends, mentors, coaches, and relationships who see what I can be and the call on my life, and who will speak truth in love, prophesy, and pour into me. Fill me with the grace and power to fulfill my commitments to You, myself, and others. In Jesus' name, Amen!*

Activation

Write out a list of the people God has placed in your life—church family, pastors, small group leaders, and close godly friends. Ask the Lord to show you anyone in your life He has placed there who you haven't understood was for accountability. Ask the Lord to speak to you about what accountability looks like in this season of your life. Write it all down and pray over what He tells you.

Ask the Lord who He would have you share your four questions revelation/answers with for accountability. Go to these people and share what the Lord has shown you about this next year of your life. Ask them to hold you accountable to walk intentionally in obedience to what He has said.

Be sure to give Him glory by giving testimony to what He does in your life! Hang on! It's going to be wild!

DAY 18: THE END OF BARRENNESS

"Sing, O barren one, who did not bear; break
forth into singing and cry aloud, you who have
not been in labor! For the children of the
desolate one will be more than the children of
her who is married," says the LORD. "Enlarge
the place of your tent, and let the curtains of
your habitations be stretched out; do not hold
back; lengthen your cords and strengthen your
stakes. For you will spread abroad to the right
and to the left, and your offspring will possess
the nations and will people the desolate cities."
Isaiah 54:1-4

Daughter, the Lord says, "I'm bringing fruitfulness in place of barrenness. I'm bringing life in place of death. I'm going to give you vindication in place of humiliation, a reversal of fortune, and a restoration of everything lost and stolen from you by your mortal enemy. I am going to do these things because You are going to influence the nations. You are going to resettle and restore abandoned cities."

Do you know what time it is? It is time to *expand*. It is time to extend your reach and stretch out in new directions—to become larger, grow vigorously, and increase in influence. It's time to get *fat*. Fat with hope. Fat with love. Fat with faith. Fat with courage and boldness. Fat with tenacity and determination. Fat with Holy Spirit vision!

Right now, right here, your barrenness is over. You are healed. Isaiah the prophet has prophesied it. Take it. It's yours! How do you take it? You sing!

Singing shifts the atmosphere inside and out (Psalm 138). It renews your joy and diminishes sorrow in the face of God's goodness. With joy comes strength (Nehemiah 8:10). With joy comes endurance (Hebrews 12:2). With joy comes *hope* (Romans 15:13)! It refocuses your attention back onto our great God, what He has done, and what He will do. It opens up your prophetic vision by celebrating future promises as present realities.

Singing is an effective weapon of war. It overcomes obstacles and the enemy. Singing releases the power of God in battle (2 Chronicles 20:22). Singing releases the power of God to open prison doors and break every chain (Acts 16:25-26).

What people, places, and circumstances need your song right now?

Prayer

> *Father, in the name of Jesus, You have commanded me to sing and shout and celebrate. Right now, fill me with joy over the victory, breakthrough, and fulfillment of every prophetic promise You have given. Put a song in my heart and in my mouth. Holy Spirit, come! Fill me with understanding of the power of this weapon of warfare. This is the day of salvation. I will rejoice and be glad in it! In Jesus' name, Amen.*

Activation

What areas in your personal life seem dry and barren? Does your body need healing? Do you need deliverance or breakthrough in habits, finances, relationships, or family? *Sing* and shout and celebrate over them, giving praise and glory to the Lord! Envision victory, breakthrough, and fulfillment. Sing in the spirit a new song in your heavenly language (tongues) and sing with your understanding songs of praise and worship. Sing songs of breakthrough, deliverance, and healing. Sing and prophesy about breakthrough and barrenness. Make a list of the people, places, and circumstances around you that need a breakthrough. Sing again!

DAY 19: SAY YES

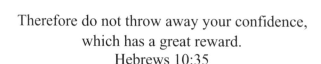

Therefore do not throw away your confidence,
which has a great reward.
Hebrews 10:35

It is the Lord who goes before you. He will be
with you; he will not leave you or forsake you.
Do not fear or be dismayed.
Deuteronomy 31:8

"How can this be? How can this possibly be? I'm just the mom from Moorpark." (Moorpark, CA was the small town where I lived.)

I must have muttered that dozens of times. I was in shock. During worship, a vision had opened up in my heart. It stunned me, frightened me, shocked me, and awed me.

I could see it so clearly in my mind. I saw the Lord seated on a throne. A story unfolded in the vision in which the Lord showed me the future of my life. I was going to be sent to the nations to speak, preach, and prophesy. I didn't see how this could happen. I didn't see how in the world God could use me. I didn't see any evidence that something like this could come to pass. I didn't see how my husband would ever agree to something like that. I felt small. I felt keenly aware of my past in all its ugliness. I felt afraid.

But I said "Yes." I simply said "Yes" and agreed to walk through any door He opened and do whatever He asked of me without question. He would have to speak to me in a way I could understand.

And God did it all. He fulfilled the vision. He will do it for you, too.

Prayer

Father, You are the God who opens and closes doors. You are the God who calls and equips. You are the God who speaks. I'm asking today to speak to me in a way that I can hear. What is it You want me to say "Yes" to? In Jesus' name, Amen.

Activation

Visions are one of the ways God speaks to His people. They are pictures that create a story. You can have visions with the naked eye, like when you watch a movie on a screen. Or you can see a vision in your mind's eye, like seeing pictures through your imagination.

Invite the Holy Spirit to bring you visions about your future. Write them down and ask Him to tell you what they mean and how you can partner with them even now.

DAY 20: WRITE THE VISION

Write the vision; make it plain on tablets,
so he may run who reads it.
For still the vision awaits its appointed time;
it hastens to the end—it will not lie.
If it seems slow, wait for it;
it will surely come; it will not delay.
Habakkuk 2:2-3

"I came that they may have life and have it
abundantly."
John 10:10

"I am created to fan the flames of revival in the
hearts of men and women in every nation,
to encourage, empower, and equip
the Body of Christ to move forward
in the call of God on their lives."
Dr. Kim Maas

Jesus came to bring life. No matter the circumstances in which He found Himself, or the people He found Himself with, He kept to that God-given vision.

Do you have a God-given vision for your life? The Lord wants to give you a vision. There is power in vision. Scripture says people become discouraged when they have no prophetic vision (Proverbs 29:18a). Life can be challenging. We face choices and decisions every day. Having a God-given vision allows us to see each decision within a bigger picture. Having a God-given vision gives us direction for the choices and decisions we make each day.

What is a prophetic vision? It is how God sees the future of your life—the outcome of the work of Christ and His Spirit in you. It speaks of what can and will be. We were all born with gifts and a calling waiting to be released within a prophetic destiny. A prophetic vision comes from God by revelation. As we reflect on our life, ask questions about our future, and seek the Lord, the Holy Spirit unfolds to us the vision God has for our lives.

Over the next few days, let's intentionally seek the Lord together for a fresh prophetic vision for your life.

Prayer

> *Father, You are a God of vision. You see me. You see my future. You know what You placed inside of me. You know my heart, my past, and my present. You know the purposes for which You created me. I am asking You to reveal Your plans and purposes to me. I am asking You to walk me through the process of receiving fresh vision for the future. I want to see what You see. I want to dream for myself what You dream for me. I want to dream for others what You dream for them and how I can be a part of that dream. I open my heart and my spirit to You, Holy Spirit. In Jesus' name, Amen.*

Activation

Invite the Holy Spirit to show you a *picture* of where you are in your life and how He sees you. Draw or describe what comes to your mind. Do not edit or analyze it. (It could be a clock, a house, an eagle, a river, a plane, etc.). Now ask the Holy Spirit what this image represents. Why this image? Why these colors? What does this mean? Write out what He shows you.

DAY 21: WRITE THE VISION— A VISION TO DIE FOR

"And who knows whether you have not come
to the kingdom for such a time as this?"
Esther 4:14

"Then I will go to the king, though it is against
the law, and if I perish, I perish."
Esther 4:16

Esther had a vision to die for, but she didn't see it until someone else showed her the bigger picture. She didn't realize she could be more until someone helped her think in a new way about who she was and about the purpose for which she had been created. She was not an ordinary girl, an orphan become queen. She was the champion of her people, God's instrument in His plan of salvation.

I want you to see the bigger picture of your life and realize you have a part to play in the kingdom of God. Each of our lives is a mission, a vision that originated from God Himself. We are anointed and appointed by God and have been sent into the families, schools, workplaces, cities, and nations to bring the kingdom—the presence, rule, and reign of Jesus the King.

Like Mordecai exhorted Esther, Laurie Beth Jones exhorts us to see the bigger kingdom picture of our lives when she writes, "Every word we speak, every action we take, has an effect on the totality of humanity. No one can escape that privilege—or responsibility."[4]

We have a privilege and a responsibility to get a vision to die for.

---

[4]Laurie Beth Jones, *The Path: Creating Your Mission Statement for Work And Life*, (New York, NY: Hatchette, 1996), 14.

Prayer

Father, give me a vision to die for! I accept my privilege and responsibility. Holy Spirit, be my Mordecai. Speak to me in ways that will awaken kingdom vision and allow me to see beyond my present circumstances. In Jesus' name, Amen.

Activation

Reflect on your life right now. Where do you work? Who are the people around you? In what city, region, or part of the nation do you live? Who is your family? Invite the Holy Spirit to speak to you about the needs and the issues represented in all these places. Which of these areas stirs your passion? Which of these needs or issues gets you angry? Journal about it.

DAY 22: WRITE THE VISION —
GIFTED AND TALENTED

Having gifts that differ according to the grace
given to us, let us use them.
Romans 12:6

I give thanks to my God always for you because
of the grace of God that was given you in Christ
Jesus, that in every way you were enriched in
him in all speech and all knowledge—even as
the testimony about Christ was confirmed
among you—so that you are not lacking in any gift.
1 Corinthians 1:4-7

For three days in the third grade, a tall, nice man came the door of my classroom and the teacher excused me to go with him to the office. There I drew, answered questions, told stories, and had conversations with the tall, nice man. I remember drawing a beautiful princess. After three days, the tall, nice man did not come to my class anymore. I had no idea why he came or why he left.

Weeks later, I found out that the tall, nice man had come to test me to see if I was "gifted and talented." The teacher thought I should be tested. My mom explained to me that kids were tested and then scored. The scores would show whether or not they were gifted and talented. Kids who scored high enough to be deemed gifted and talented were promoted in the classroom. They had special classes, reading, homework, and privileges. Since they were gifted and talented, somehow they were special.

My score fell short by half a point. The tall, nice man told my mom that if I worked very hard, I could probably keep up with the gifted kids, but I was not gifted and talented.

How many of us have been told by the devil that we are not special, gifted, or talented? How many of us never attempt to go to college, apply for a promotion, or ask for something more out of life because we have believed we don't have what it takes and never will? How many of us have believed the lie that we have nothing to give and can never be used to fulfill a vision of God?

God says otherwise.

Prayer

> *Father, You say that I am gifted and talented because You are in me and I am in You. The Holy Spirit has been poured out on all flesh—that means I qualify! The Holy Spirit in me is the greatest gift and with Him comes His supernatural gifts and power. Baptize me in Your Spirit right now! I reject and come out of alignment with any lie from the enemy that says I have no gift, no talent, and no hope of becoming more than I am right now. I break the power of every lie I have believed from the time I was a child that does not line up with Your Word of truth. I want to think of myself the way You think of me. I want to see myself the way You see me. I want to envision my life in the light of Your vision for me. Come Holy Spirit! In Jesus' name, Amen.*

Activation

Ask your closest friends to answer this question: "Knowing me, what are the things you would say I am good at?" Write their responses down in your journal. Then, write your own list of at least ten things you are good at.

Lastly, what spiritual gifts do you desire to see in operation in your life? Ask the Holy Spirit to impart them to you right now. How will you begin to develop and grow these gifts in your life? Write it all down and commit it to the Lord.

DAY 23: WRITE THE VISION—PUZZLE PIECES

And we know that for those who love God all
things work together for good, for those who are
called according to his purpose.
Romans 8:28

And the angel of the Lord appeared to him in a
flame of fire out of the midst of a bush. He
looked, and behold, the bush was burning, yet it
was not consumed. And Moses said, "I will turn
aside to see this great sight, why the bush is not
burned." When the Lord saw that he turned
aside to see, God called to him out of the bush,
"Moses, Moses!" And he said, "Here I am." . . .
"And now, behold, the cry of the people of
Israel has come to me, and I have also seen the
oppression with which the Egyptians oppress
them. Come, I will send you to Pharaoh that you
may bring my people, the children of Israel, out
of Egypt."
Exodus 3:2-4, 9-10

When Moses received His God-vision, it put together all the pieces of the puzzle of His life. He was born into a priestly family. His life had been threatened. He was saved by Pharaoh's daughter, which allowed him to be raised as royalty with the finest education, knowledge of the culture, and the government leadership of his time. Then he discovered his roots. He stepped out in the flesh and killed a man. He was rejected, demoted, displaced, and thrown into the wilderness. He learned the ways of a shepherd and nomadic life. He became content with the back side of the desert where there was no privilege or power, no pomp and circumstance. But he had a staff. And God had a plan.

A God-vision for your life puts together all the pieces of your puzzle. Nothing is wasted. Every season, all acquired skill and knowledge, and every event in the past and the present are useful to God. Life is full of twists and turns. The journey leading to vision and from vision is never a straight line. What seems like random pieces of life are pieces to the puzzle that, when put together, create a grand vision.

We must look at the whole of our life through prophetic lenses to see what God sees. Prophetic perspective allows us to see from heaven's perspective. We see what is in light of what will be.

Prayer

> *Father, my life is not an accident. Even when I have made choices on my own, You have been watching, waiting, orchestrating, and working all things together for good in my life. Thank You! Holy Spirit, come and begin to show me how everything ties together. I ask You, in the name of Jesus, to put the pieces together of my past and present to give me a God-vision of the future. In Jesus' name, Amen.*

Activation

Spend some time in the presence of the Lord. Invite the Holy Spirit to take you through the seasons in your life, beginning with childhood. What were your interests? What did you dream of being when you grew up? What is the history of your family related to dreams and ministry and gifting? What was your favorite class? What talents, passions, and interests have you inherited from each of your family members? What jobs and professions have you held in your life?

Have you ever had a "burning bush" experience when you encountered the Holy Spirit and you heard God's voice? What did He say? Write it all down and then invite the Holy Spirit to put the pieces together. Write down what He reveals.

DAY 24: WRITE THE VISION— FINDING PASSION FOR MISSION

And I heard the voice of the Lord saying,
"Whom shall I send, and who will go for us?"
Then I said, "Here I am! Send me."
And he said, "Go…"
Isaiah 6:8-9a

Today, you are going look into your heart and listen to its passion. If God has knit you together in your mother's womb, knows your going out and coming in, works everything together for your good, put eternity in your heart, and lives within your heart by His Spirit, then the passions of your heart also belong to Him (Psalm 139, Romans 8:28, Ecclesiastes 3:11, John 15-16).

Godly passion points to your mission and sustains vision. It gives you a clue to what God has placed in your heart to do. It keeps you going when the way gets hard. Joy and endurance for the journey are partners with passion. Jesus was passionate about His mission: "for the joy set before him, he endured the cross . . ." (Hebrews 12:2).

Today, take a risk and dare to discover the passion the Lord has cultivated in your heart.

Prayer

Father, in the name of Jesus, I silence the voice of the enemy and the voice of my flesh. Holy Spirit, reveal to me today what I created for, what my heart is truly passionate about. Again, I say, here am I, send me! In Jesus' name, Amen.

Activation

With journal in hand, invite the Holy Spirit to come manifest His presence and open your heart, your ears, and your eyes. Then, answer the questions below.

- ☐ If you were ten times bolder and money, time, and education were no problem, what would you be doing with your life?
- ☐ What most excites you, most saddens you, and most angers you in the world?
- ☐ If you had the power to change anything in your city, nation, or the world, what would it be?
- ☐ If you could choose any people group, age group, or geographical place to be an influence for God, who and where would you choose?
- ☐ What practical need do people in the world have that you would fulfill if you had the resources?
- ☐ What spiritual need do people in the world have that you would fulfill if you had the resources?
- ☐ What three action words describe the deepest passion of your heart?
- ☐ What three action words does the Holy Spirit say describe the deepest passion of your heart? (For example, mine are "encourage, empower, and equip"!)
- ☐ Is there anything going on in the world, any injustice or cause, that you would be willing to give your voice and your life to, even if it meant losing your life (a vision to die for)?

Write all the answers down. Ask the Holy Spirit to speak to you about your heart and how He loves you.

DAY 25: WRITE THE VISION—SAY YES!

And Jesus said to them, "Follow me,
and I will make you become fishers of men."
And *immediately* they left their nets
and followed him.
Mark 1:17-18

The disciples were not disciples until they said "Yes" to the vision and mission Jesus had for them.

For several years, I pastored in the local church. Many of the folks in my church would tell you they were disciples, yet they were not saying "Yes" to following Jesus. They had said "Yes" to the American dream, to seeking success in their job or among their peers, and to going to church.

We were created for more. Jesus died on the cross and shed His precious blood on our behalf to save us from our sin, reconcile us to God, and restore us to the call of God on our lives. He died so that we could be made ready to receive the Holy Spirit and power. Why? So that as citizens of the kingdom of God, we would be empowered to demonstrate the kingdom wherever we go—pushing back darkness, healing the sick, casting out demons, raising the dead, preaching the gospel to all creation, and bringing the love of Christ to all.

The God-vision we have been seeking in the last several days will be unique to each of us because we are each uniquely created by God. Even so, it is the call of God to fulfill His purposes on the earth. He is calling.

It is time to put it all together. Once you have put it all together, and have your fresh God-vision, you are responsible to decide whether you will say "Yes." Saying "Yes" means following Jesus as He empowers you by the Holy Spirit to fulfill the vision.

Prayer

Father, today I am asking You to help me put it all together, everything we have discovered together the last few days. Reveal to me my unique God-vision and mission. You called the fishermen to become fishers of men. What are You calling me to? In Jesus' name, Amen.

Activation

Invite the Holy Spirit to come and open your ears and eyes. Take out all the notes you have written over the last several days as you have sought the Lord for fresh vision. Read over all your answers.

- ☐ Ask the Holy Spirit to highlight for you three of the action words you have already chosen. Write them down.
- ☐ Ask the Holy Spirit to highlight to you the practical need, spiritual need, injustice, and cause you wrote about that is His heart for you. How do they relate to each other? Can they be combined into one or two issues or needs? If not, ask the Holy Spirit to choose one or two that are most important to His heart.
- ☐ Ask the Holy Spirit to highlight to you the one people or place of those you wrote about that are on His heart for you.
- ☐ Take all of these above and write out one sentence beginning with the words, "I am created to . . ." Keep it concise and cohesive.

Example: "I am created to fan the flames of revival in the hearts of men and women in every nation, and to encourage, empower, and equip the Body of Christ to move forward in the call of God on their lives." (Dr. Kim Maas)

It may take you a few days to find the right combination of words before you get the sense that it is the right fit. Just as with a prophetic word, you should feel a witness in your spirit about the vision statement. Share it with a close friend or a leader who knows you, and allow them to help if you need it.

Once you have your God-vision, give it to the Lord in prayer and say your "Yes."

DAY 26: WRITE THE VISION—
PROPHESY THE VISION

And as I prophesied, there was a sound, and
behold, a rattling, and the bones came together,
bone to its bone. And I looked, and behold,
there were sinews on them, and flesh had come
upon them, and skin had covered them. But
there was no breath in them. Then he said to me,
"Prophesy to the breath; prophesy, son of man,
and say to the breath, Thus says the Lord God:
Come from the four winds, O breath, and
breathe on these slain, that they may live." So I
prophesied as he commanded me, and the breath
came into them, and they lived and stood on
their feet, an exceedingly great army.
Ezekiel 37: 7-10

Prophecy and vision go together. Prophecy declares the fulfillment of the vision. When we are shown by the Lord what He wants to accomplish, we can prophesy and declare that it is done. Agreeing with God's words in this way releases creative power, because God's words are never empty words—they are words that are always fulfilled.

Ezekiel prophesies the vision of God's exceedingly great army. At the time, they seemed like dry bones, but our God is the God of the present and future. He asked Ezekiel to prophesy the future: the vision of the time when God's plan and purpose would come to fulfillment.

Now that you have written your God-vision, it is time to envision the time when the vision is fulfilled. Then prophesy it over your life!

Prayer

Father, You know the future and the present. You said the Holy Spirit would show us the things to come (John 15:12). I lift up the vision You have helped me write for my life, and I ask You to show me what my life will look like when it comes to fulfillment. Holy Spirit come, fill me afresh and open my ears to hear You. Tell me what is to come. In the name of Jesus, amen.

Activation

With journal in hand, invite the Holy Spirit to help you see what your life will look like when God's purposes for your life are fulfilled. What will you be doing? What kind of person will you be? What Scriptures will have been fulfilled in your life? What prophecies will have been fulfilled and how will have they changed you, your relationships, and your work? What will your daily work, family life, and ministry be?

Write it all down. Then prophesy it over yourself! Read it out loud and pray it back to the Lord for the next thirty days. Watch your life begin to line up with God's vision!

DAY 27: TURN EVERY CURSE INTO BLESSING

> . . . the Lord your God turned the curse
> into a blessing for you because
> the Lord your God loves you.
> Deuteronomy 23:5

> Like a sparrow in its flitting, like a swallow in its flying,
> a curse that is causeless does not alight.
> Proverbs 26:2

In Deuteronomy 23, we read about a prophet hired by a pagan king to go and curse Israel. Three times, he tried to curse them. Three times, the Lord turned the curse into a blessing.

Have you ever had someone speak a curse over your life? We all have. Sometimes we simply haven't recognized the words for what they were—a curse. Any word that doesn't agree with what The Lord says about us, our family, city, region, or nation is a curse. Negative words, such as, "You are good for nothing," or "You are going to fail and lose everything," are curses.

Sometimes we are guilty of speaking curses over our own lives. Usually this happens because someone we once looked up to spoke it to or over us at one time in our life and we believed what they said. Sometimes we have been exposed to people who operate in witchcraft, sorcery, or the occult and they have placed a curse on our lives, or on the people, places, or circumstances we care about.

You were created to live under the blessing of the Lord. You don't have time to live under a curse. What's even more important is that God is bigger than that! The Lord loves you. He sent His only Son to die, bearing your sins—the causes that allow a curse to "alight" or come upon you. The cause, the open door, for a curse to come upon you has been removed, shut, and no longer exists. What's more, because the Lord loves you, He will turn every curse into a blessing. He will do it for you, and He will do it for you on behalf of others.

Just ask Him!

Prayer

Father! You are the majestic God, the Lord Almighty, the great I Am. Nothing and no one is like You, and nothing and no one can stand against You. You are with me, You are for me, and You have declared that out of Your love for me, You will turn every curse into a blessing. Lord, in the name of Jesus Christ, I come out of agreement with any word spoken over my life that has become a curse and limited my potential to fulfill the purposes for which You created me. I appropriate the shed blood of Jesus for my life. I declare that every cause that has become an open door for curses to operate in my life has been removed and cleansed by the blood of Jesus. Now, by the power of Jesus' name and His shed blood, I take authority over every hex, vex, and incantation, every form of witchcraft and every kind of curse that has been spoken or activated against me by the enemy, and I break its power. I command every curse to be made null and void and every operation, effect, and demonic attachment to be completely removed and sent back to the pit from where it originated. In the mighty name of Jesus! Now Father, in the name of Jesus, come and bring blessing into every place in my life where a curse once took up dominion. Thank You, Jesus! Amen!

Activation

Now, invite the Holy Spirit to bring to your mind the negative words and curses that have been spoken over you. Ask Him to show you the blessing He desires to bring to you in their place. Write them down and declare them over your life, beginning with the words, "I am blessed by God with/to/for _____."

Repeat the prayer and the activation on behalf of your loved ones, church, finances, business, city, and nation.

❮◇❯

DAY 28: GIRL POWER

Sometimes, when we add up all we are up
against, all the challenges before us, all the work
that lies ahead, all the problems and decisions,
the heart aches and heartbreaks, all the
downright evil, and then we add up what we've
got . . . well, it can seem a bit discouraging.
It can seem that we may as well play it
small and settle. [5]
Heidi Neumark

I therefore, a prisoner for the Lord, urge you to
walk in a manner worthy of the calling to which
you have been called . . .
Ephesians 4:1

Wonder Woman is a great movie. It is the story of a girl who has divine power, but doesn't know how powerful she really is. She understands there is a call on her life She has spent her life being trained and prepared to be a ruler, a queen. She has worked hard. She is strong, beautiful, and brilliant. She is a warrior. What she has yet to discover is the power she has been given.

As the story unfolds, we meet the enemy of her world. He is dark and foreboding. He desires control of everything in order to rule and reign supreme. His plan is for destruction and devastation. Love awakens the call on her life and Wonder Woman begins to understand her true purpose. She will stand against darkness and this dark ruler.

The battle begins. So many around her courageously are giving themselves to fight an impossible battle in the hopes some will be spared. Those she loves are being torn apart. She is being overcome and it looks like she will be

---

[5] https://www.lstc.edu/lstc-life/chapel/sermons/details-6, Accessed May 25, 2018.

beaten. The enemy will have his way. And then it happens. A power she was unaware of bursts forth from somewhere on the inside and the battle turns.

It's just a movie. Or is it?

It's time for GIRL POWER! The Bible is full of the stories of powerful women. History is full of the stories of powerful women. They were beautiful, brilliant, valiant, courageous, and powerful. Over the next few days, we are going to allow God to speak to us about them and receive and impartation from their lives.

Why? Because now is not the time to play small and settle for less than the call of God on our lives!

Prayer

> *Father, in the name of Jesus, I ask that today You would begin to make me aware of powerful women who love You with all of their hearts and serve You powerfully. Cause me to see, read, meet, and think about the women who are influencing not only their families, but also their regions, nations, and history! Stir up my passion and give me a hunger to rise up in the power of the Holy Spirit and fulfill the purposes on my own life so that your kingdom may come on earth as it is in heaven! In Jesus' name, Amen.*

Activation

Think about the women in your life. Who inspires you the most? Why? Ask the Holy Spirit to show you any place in your life where you have been playing small and settling for less. Ask Him to show you what He wants to change.

DAY 29: GIRL POWER—ESTHER

And the king said to her, "What is it, Queen Esther?
What is your request? It shall be given
you, even to the half of my kingdom."
And Esther said, "If it please the king,
let the king and Haman come today to a feast that I
have prepared for the king."
Esther 5:3-4

And Haman said to himself, "Whom would the
king delight to honor more than me?"
Esther 6:6b

This is no Cinderella story. This is not a story about beauty, romance, or going from rags to riches. This is a story about political intrigue and ethnic cleansing. It is a story about racism, bigotry, and injustice. It is a story about how God raised up a woman of integrity and humility to save an entire race.

You know the story. Her real name was Hadassah, but they called her Esther. She was an orphan being raised in a foreign land by her cousin, Mordecai. Because she was beautiful, she was taken, without a choice, into the custody of the palace for the pleasure of the pagan king. After a year of preparation, if she pleased the king, she could be chosen as queen. It didn't matter if she wanted to or not. It didn't matter if it didn't work out for her. It didn't matter if she loved him or not. She had no control over her circumstances.

The time comes when the evil man Haman plots to kill her could and all the Jews. The news comes to Esther, and Mordecai says those famous words: "Who know but that you have come to position for such a time as this." Esther decides to go to the king, though it may cost her life if it displeases him.

When she goes to the king, he offers to grant her request. It is here that Esther does a strange thing. She invites the king and her enemy to come to a feast she has prepared. What is happening here? Esther is humbling herself to serve the king with honor first. She is so brilliant and politically savvy! Before asking for something for herself, she first offers herself in service and honor. She refuses to use her position for selfish gain. She refuses to take advantage of the relationship she has with the king for selfish ambition. She chooses to honor the one in leadership even in the face of personal injustice.

Read the verses above again. The stunning wisdom of Esther's response is contrasted with Haman's thoughts. Both Esther and Haman are being given favor by the king. Both are welcome in the king's court. Both respond to the king's favor. The Scripture points out that Haman is filled with pride, while Esther is filled with humility. Haman is consumed with receiving honor for himself, while Esther chooses to give honor for the benefit of others.

What is the end result? Haman loses his life. Esther saves a nation.

We may not have control over unjust situations and circumstances in our lives, but we have control over how we will respond. How we respond will affect the lives of those around us. Honoring others opens the door to influence.

Prayer

> *Father God, You have a plan and a purpose for my life. You care about the injustice, bigotry, and racial prejudice people face. Yet Your way is the way of humility, service, and honor. Teach me Your ways. Position me to honor well when I receive favor. Use me to honor and speak to leaders who have authority to save nations. In Jesus' name, Amen.*

Activation

Who are the leaders in your life? Pray for them and invite the Holy Spirit to speak to you about ways in which you can show them honor.

DAY 30: GIRL POWER—THE HEBREW MIDWIVES

> Then the king of Egypt said to the Hebrew
> midwives . . . "When you serve as midwife to
> the Hebrew women and see them on the birth-
> stool, if it is a son, you shall kill him, but if it is
> a daughter, she shall live." But the midwives
> feared God and did not do as the king of Egypt
> commanded them . . . So God dealt well with
> the midwives. And the people multiplied and
> grew very strong. And because the midwives
> feared God, he gave them families.
> Exodus 1: 16-21

I was ministering in Brazil. I had just stepped down from the platform and followed the interpreter to the back room. Just as I was about to sit down, the door opened and a dark-haired man entered the room. He was looking for me. Through an interpreter, he said he was a prophet and the Lord had sent him to me. I nodded and gave him permission to speak.

He said, "The Lord knows your heart, that you miss your children and that you have paid a price in your family to minister to the nations. You will gain favor in this country and in many more nations, but the Lord says because you have said yes to care for His children, He will care for your children. Thus says the Lord."

I have written the word given to me as closely as I can remember it. I remember tears coming to my eyes. It was a true word and it reassured me that my family, my children, were best cared for when I was walking in the fear of the Lord fulfilling His will for my life.

I love my family. Family has always been the greatest desire of my heart. I have a husband, three grown children, and five grandsons. They are important to me. At each stage in my life I have been mindful of how I was serving the Lord in ministry in order to keep those relationships strong. Yet, in the fear of the Lord, I never turned away from the call on my life. It has not been easy.

Because the midwives feared God, He gave them families, the Scripture says. A family was the desire of their heart. If we want families that are strong, powerful, and walking with the Lord, then we need to fear God, serve Him only and completely, and not give in to the lies of the enemy or the ways of the culture.

The Hebrew midwives did not try to save their own lives. They cared for God's people and fulfilled the purpose and call on their lives. They were midwives. They helped deliver babies. They knew the Lord called them to bring life into the world. When their lives were threatened, when their families were at stake, they did not quit and run away. They feared the Lord and continued to say "Yes" to the call. And God gave them the desire of their heart. He gave them a legacy of life.

God has a purpose for you to fulfill. As you obey Him, He will care for everything that concerns you, including your family. Perhaps a family is the desire of your heart and you have not seen that desire fulfilled. Is the Lord is waiting for you to say yes to His purposes for your life?

Prayer

Father, You already know what it means to my life and the lives of those I love to say "Yes" to Your will. I will not allow the enemy to tell me that if I fulfill the call on my life, I will die and my family will suffer. You can give me wisdom. You can watch over and care for my family. You can give me the time and the strategy to have a family and fulfill the purposes for which I was created. Because I choose to fear You, You will deal well with me and give me my family as a gift for my heart. Thank You, Father. You are so, so good to me.

Activation

Invite the Holy Spirit to help you reflect on your life. Are you living in the fear of the Lord, serving His purposes? Are you willing to say "yes" today? Spend some time searching your heart and then tell God what you have decided.

At every stage of a woman's life, she has a responsibility to care for her family. God expects us to fulfill our responsibilities in the home. However, He can give us a strategy for how to fulfill the call of God on our lives without neglecting those responsibilities. Ask the Holy Spirit to give you a strategy for this stage of your life that will keep family relationships strong while serving the Lord.

DAY 31: GIRL POWER—HAGAR

And he said, "Hagar, servant of Sarai, where
have you come from and where are you going?"
She said, "I am fleeing from my mistress Sarai."
The angel of the Lord said to her, "Return to
your mistress and submit to her . . . And the
angel of the Lord said to her, "Behold, you are
pregnant and shall bear a son. You shall call his
name Ishmael, because the Lord has listened to
your affliction."
Genesis 16: 8-9

So she called the name of the Lord who spoke to
her, "You are a God of seeing," for she said,
"Truly here I have seen him who looks after
me."
Genesis 16:13

God sees. And God gives us eyes to see what He sees. This is what Hagar discovers, and it gives her strength to do the hard thing—to go back to a difficult situation and be submitted to a leadership that is jealous and insecure because of what she is carrying.

Sarai could not have children, and in a desperate move to try and bring fulfillment to a prophetic promise from God, she makes a decision that is of the flesh and not the spirit. She gives her servant Hagar to her husband to have a child. It works. Hagar conceives. Hagar didn't ask for this. She didn't have a choice. She was a victim of her circumstances. Then she mistakenly thinks her status is now elevated and her attitude changes toward her leader. Sarai over-reacts and treats her "harshly."

So, Hagar runs away. Out in the desert, dry, weary, and alone, Hagar is visited by God. She wasn't looking for Him. The only thing she saw was her circumstances. But God saw. And God heard. God knew her affliction, but He also knew something she did not know. God knew her future. God knew the whole of her life in ways she did not, and could not, know. God tells her what He alone knew about the future so that she could bear up under the present and do the hard thing He was asking of her: "Return to your mistress and submit . . ."

God sees. When God gives us eyes to see what He sees by prophetically revealing our future to us, we gain the strength to do the hard things. Running from the challenges, trials, and difficulties in the present can cause us to forfeit the promises of God in our lives. God has more for us than this. Eternity is waiting, and this present suffering is nothing in comparison to that. But it is not only eternity that awaits us. There are specific prophetic promises God has for us for our future in this life.

We need to know the God of Hagar—the God of seeing who looks after us.

Prayer

Father God, You are the God of seeing. You see the past, present, and future of my life. You are looking after me, seeing my present circumstances for what they are with the understanding of where they are leading and how they will work out for the future. Look after me. See me. And give me eyes to see You and know You as the God of seeing. Reveal to me what You alone can see about my life and the lives of those to whom You are sending me. Thank You for seeing me. Thank You for looking after me. Tell me what I must do in every circumstance to receive the future You have planned for me. In Jesus' name, Amen.

Activation

Invite the Holy Spirit to open your eyes to see your current circumstances the way God sees them. Ask Him to give you a prophetic understanding of what is ahead that will give you the strength to do whatever He is asking you to do. Write it down. Are there adjustments in your decisions and actions that need to be made for you to be in agreement with and in obedience to this word?

Invite the Holy Spirit to bring to your mind a friend who is going through a difficult situation and wants to quit or run away from it. Ask Him to give you a picture, word, or Scripture that will reveal to them the promises of God for their future. Ask the Holy Spirit to speak to you about how this word, picture, or Scripture will give them strength to continue on in their circumstances.

DAY 32: GIRL POWER—SARAH, PART I

And God said to Abraham, "As for Sarai your
wife, you shall not call her name Sarai, but
Sarah shall be her name. I will bless her, and
moreover, I will give you a son by her. I will
bless her, and she shall become nations; kings of
peoples shall come from her . . ."
Genesis 17:15-16

The Lord said to Abraham, "Why did Sarah
laugh and say, 'Shall I indeed bear a child,
now that I am old?'
Is anything too hard for the Lord?"
Genesis 18:13

"At the appointed time I will return to you,
about this time next year,
and Sarah shall have a son."
Genesis 18:14

Whenever God changes a name in Scripture, it is because He is calling the person into their true identity. Sarai, which means "princess," will now be Sarah, "queen" or "mother of nations." She was royalty from the beginning, but she is being called to rise up and stand alongside Abraham, the "father of nations." Her destiny was never to be a tag-along, someone who accompanies but is not invited to have any significant role in the plan. Sarah is receiving her call, an invitation to partnership for the sake of the kingdom of God.

Part of her calling is to be the vessel through which the prophetic promise of God will come. She will bear a son. It is not something she can do in her own strength—she cannot fake it, think it, or even conceive it into being. She can only open up her heart and life and yield to it. She will have to allow herself to become completely vulnerable to the word of the Lord and His will for her life. It will be God's doing if it comes into being. How will she respond?

She laughs. She responds with doubt and unbelief. She comes to a defining moment.

God asks, "*Is anything too hard for me?*" The Hebrew word for "hard" in this passage can be translated "wonderful." God is asking Sarah, "Is anything to wonderful for me to do for you? Am I good enough, in your understanding of me, to do this wonderful thing in, for, and through you? Is it bigger than me, better than me, greater than what I am capable of?"

There comes a moment in all of our lives, if we are daring to follow Jesus, when we will either take a stand to believe God's word, heart, kindness, and ability to fulfill the promise, or we shrink back.

Isaiah said, "If you are not firm in faith, you will not be firm at all" (Isaiah 7:9). Paul said, "Be on guard. Stand firm in the faith. Be courageous. Be strong" (1 Corinthians 16:13 NLT). The writer of Hebrews says:

> Therefore do not throw away your confidence, which has a great reward. For you have need of endurance, so that when you have done the will of God you may receive what is promised. For, "Yet a little while, and the coming one will come and will not delay; but my righteous one shall live by faith, and if he shrinks back, my soul has no pleasure in him." But we are not of those who shrink back and are destroyed, but of those who have faith and preserve their souls. (Hebrews 10:35-39)

Sarah finds a place to stand in faith and accepts the invitation. How do I know? She conceived a son, which means after years of barrenness, years of staggering disappointment and pain, and growing through menopause, Sarah had sexual relations with Abraham. As women, we can understand the meaning of this. So many of us, myself included, have been through the pain of miscarriage, or barrenness.

We understand Sarah in this guarded moment. And we can imagine what would be required to offer up such worship unto God. This precious and costly act of worship, this faith-filled vulnerability to the word of the Lord, releases the power and favor of God over her life and she conceives.

It is the working of God met by yieldedness in us that gives birth to prophetic promise. This yieldedness in us requires that we let go of self-protecting and the insistance on being in control. This allows God's power to be released in us to shape us to become who we were created to be.

Prayer

> *Father God, I want to become who You created me to be. I want to rise up into the call on my life. I want Your promises for me to come to pass. If there is anywhere in my life where pain or suffering has caused me to take control of my life, or doubt and disbelieve that You could do wonderful things for me, please forgive me, heal me, and help me believe. I am making a decision right now to yield and surrender in an act of worship to Your Word, your promises, and the prophetic words over my life. I believe nothing is too hard or wonderful for You to do. In Jesus' name, Amen.*

Activation

Invite the Holy Spirit to give you a name that best describes who you really are. Write it down and research it. Where does your heart struggle to believe it and why? What thoughts and actions will you need to stop or start having if you are to walk in agreement with this spiritual name from the Lord? Write it down and make an action plan.

Think about the people in your life. Do the above activation on their behalf. Consider prophesying over them with the understanding you have gained by the Holy Spirit.

DAY 33: GIRL POWER—SARAH, PART II

But Sarah saw the son of Hagar the Egyptian,
whom she had borne to Abraham, laughing. So
she said to Abraham, "Cast out this slave
woman with her son, for the son of this slave
woman shall not be heir with my son Isaac."
Genesis 21:9-10

But God said to Abraham, "Be not displeased
because of the boy and because of your slave
woman. Whatever Sarah says to you, do as she
tells you, for through Isaac shall your offspring
be named."
Genesis 21:12

Now you, brothers, like Isaac, are children of
promise. But just as at that time he who was
born according to the flesh persecuted him who
was born according to the Spirit, so also it is
now.
But what does the Scripture say? "Cast out the
slave woman and her son, for the son of the
slave woman shall not inherit with the son of the
free woman."
Galatians 4:28-30

Yesterday, Sarah accepted her true identity, but the story is not finished. Not only was Sarah's identity redefined—her call and purpose were also redefined.

Now Sarah sees herself in a new way. She is no longer the barren woman. She is the mother of the promise fulfilled, the mother of nations. Now Sarah sees in a new way. She sees from a new perspective or vantage point. She sees from heaven's perspective.

Genesis says, "Sarah saw the son of Hagar the Egyptian, whom she had borne to Abraham, laughing." The Hebrew word for laughing can mean "mocking," or as some Jewish scholars translate it, "abusing" or "molesting." Paul in Galatians writes that Ishmael was persecuting Isaac.

No longer a victim of circumstance, insecure, or intimidated, Sarah stands in her identity as the mother of promise, the mother of nations, and speaks up.

Even her speech has changed. She commands, "Cast out this slave woman with her son, for the son of this slave woman shall not be heir with my son Isaac." She is using deliverance language, the kind of words we would use to cast out a demon. There will be no tolerance or compromise. There is to be a complete severance. It is the same language used when God delivered Israel from Pharaoh in Egypt.

Sarah takes back her voice, and with it, her power, authority, and God-given place in the kingdom. She is acting as the free woman of faith mentioned by Paul in Galatians and she will not allow the promises of God in her life to be enslaved, corrupted, mocked, stolen, or destroyed. She understood that Ishmael as the firstborn could lay claim to Abraham's wealth and property by cultural laws. Sarah understood what was at stake. The God-given promises, the God-given inheritance, the God-given name, were not to be stolen by Egypt, but preserved for the kingdom of God.

Through she was a woman in a patriarchal society, the Lord backed her up telling Abraham, "Whatever Sarah says to you, do as she tells you."

Wait. We've heard this before! This is what Mary says to the servants at the wedding at Cana: "Whatever he says to you, do it" (John 2:5). Sarah is a type of Christ in this story. God has taken this marginalized woman with a past full of reproach, shame, and barrenness, and given her governmental authority to lead her tribe in order to protect His promises for their lives.

Sarah is the freewoman of faith. She is the mother of nations. The story does not end there, because thousands of years later, we, like countless other women from generation to generation, are reading her story. I am recalling the story of Sarah's life to remind you of who you are. Jesus has delivered you from slavery and bondage. It is for freedom that He has set you free. He has secured for you a place in the covenant promises of God for this time.

I am here to remind you of the heritage, identity, and freedom that are already yours, paid for in full by Jesus Christ.

I am here to remind you of the call on your life.

I am here to remind you that the Holy Spirit has been poured out and you are a new creation.

I am here to remind you that you belong to a people of the Spirit with miracle-working power and authority.

I am here to remind you to take back your voice, your power, and your authority in Christ and use them to deliver God's people from their bondage, so that the prophetic promises of God are preserved in their lives.

We are Sarah's daughters. We are in a moment in history when God is about to raise up a mighty company of women to participate in an unprecedented move of God. Are you ready?

Prayer

> *Father God, I am not who the enemy says I am, who the culture says I am, or who the past says I am. I am who You say I am. I have Your life, Your mind, Your Spirit, and Your power. I have the name of Jesus, the promises of Scripture, and weapons of warfare that are mighty for pulling down strongholds. I am called, anointed, and appointed for this hour. I accept the call. Here I am, Lord. Send me! In Jesus' name, Amen!*

Activation

Spend some time in worship. Soak in God's presence. Invite the Holy Spirit to reveal to you any place in your life where there is still a "bondwoman" that needs to be cast out. It can be old wounds, mindsets, bad habits, unhealthy relationships, sin, or bondage of any kind. Sarah was uncompromising and deliberate. Ask the Holy Spirit to give you an uncompromising spirit regarding this bondage and to deliver you from it. Ask Him if there is any unforgiveness or affections causing you to hold on to it. If there is, ask Him how to forgive and let it all go. Then ask Him to lead you and guide you in a prayer to "throw out the bondwoman."

Think about the people God has placed in your life and how you can help them throw out their bondwoman. Ask the Holy Spirit to give you a strategy and an opportunity to lovingly and gently help them through it.

DAY 34: GIRL POWER—DEBORAH

> In the days of Shamgar, son of Anath, in the
> days of Jael, the highways were abandoned, and
> travelers kept to the byways. The villagers
> ceased in Israel; they ceased to be until I arose;
> I, Deborah, arose as a mother in Israel.
> Judges 5:6-7

> Barak said to her, "If you will go with me, I will
> go, but if you will not go with me, I will not
> go." And she said, "I will surely go with you.
> Nevertheless, the road on which you are going
> will not lead to your glory, for the Lord will sell
> Sisera into the hand of a woman." Then
> Deborah arose and went with Barak to Kedesh.
> And Barak called out Zebulun and Naphtali to
> Kedesh. And 10,000 men went up at his heels,
> and Deborah went up with him.
> Judges 4:8-10

Deborah is one of my favorite female heroines. A prophet in my country once asked me which of the prophets in the Bible could I relate to. He mentioned Moses, Elijah, and John the Baptist. I said, "Deborah." Sometimes we forget that she is in the company of prophets and judges that led all of Israel. Her leadership was prophetic, fearless, and decisive. She served in a governmental role over the entire nation. She commanded the commander of the armies of Israel. She told him what enemy to face and where and when to do it. She rode out to battle with the leaders and the troops. She went to war alongside men. And she fulfilled her God-given leadership role as a female without apology.

Leadership is a calling of God. It is not male or female. Deborah was called to rise up as a mother in Israel. The result of her answering the call to leadership was the return of safety and prosperity and godly rule to an entire region. When Scripture says the highways were abandoned, travelers kept to the byways, and villagers ceased, it is describing the dangerous, corrupt, crime-ridden culture in the region. When Deborah arose, life returned and people no longer had to live in survival mode—they could begin to thrive.

Deborah was a prophet, judge, warrior, and leader. This is what it meant to be a mother in Israel. Israel, its people and villages, were her children given into her care by God. Her leadership improved their lives in every way. She didn't shrink back from the call of leadership on her life.

There is an unprecedented call going out from the Lord to raise up Deborah's right now. What does this mean? God is looking for women who will see people, cities, and nations as their children and take action in response to the enemy's destructive plans and works against them. God is calling many women into leadership, both inside and outside the church. We are all, male and female, called to go out to war against the world of darkness that is causing villagers to cease, and the highways and byways to be abandoned.

Those of us called to leadership must do so without fear, without offense, and without apology. We must neither usurp our brothers nor abandon them. We must stand with them and take our stand against our common enemy.

Prayer

> *Father God, our people, our cities, and our nation need leaders who will restore safety, prosperity, and godly rule. We need leaders who will be fearless and hear the voice of the Lord, judge matters in righteousness, and stand against our true enemy. Raise up these kinds of leaders, male and female. Restore fathers and mothers to care for all people. If You desire to use me in a leadership role, prepare my heart and give me the ability to see where the enemy has plagued my people, my neighborhood, and my nation, and give me the wisdom, prophetic insight, and power to do something about it. In Jesus' name, Amen!*

Activation

Invite the Holy Spirit to show you your own area of influence. Ask Him to show you how to be a "mother" in that area, whether it is to one person or many, one house or many. Ask Him to speak to you about your household and your neighborhood and show you where life has ceased. Then invite Him to show you the actions you can take to restore safety, prosperity, and godly rule.

DAY 35: GIRL POWER—JAEL

And Jael came out to meet Sisera and said to
him, "Turn aside, my lord; turn aside to me; do
not be afraid." So he turned aside to her into the
tent, and she covered him with a rug. And he
said to her, "Please give me a little water to
drink, for I am thirsty." So she opened a skin of
milk and gave him a drink and covered him.
And he said to her, "Stand at the opening of the
tent, and if any man comes and asks you, 'Is
anyone here?' say, 'No.'" But Jael the wife of
Heber took a tent peg, and took a hammer in her
hand. Then she went softly to him and drove the
peg into his temple until it went down into the
ground while he was lying fast asleep from
weariness. So he died.
Judges 4:18-21

Jael didn't kill Sisera because he was a man. She killed him because he was
evil, and when evil came near her tent, she took authority over it and drove a
tent peg through its head! She didn't wait till her husband came home. She
didn't compromise with him or hope, beg, or politely ask him to go. She
didn't ask questions and wait to hear what he had to say. She did not open
herself or her household to this evil. She put an end to his invasion into her
domain. She took dominion over evil and protected what God had placed
under her authority. She knew which side she was on, and she wasn't going to
play politics with evil. She killed him. Dead. In her tent. Done.

Hopefully you get the point. We all have been given a sphere of authority that
includes our personal lives, bodies, families, relationships, finances, identity,
calling, and the places and people God has given us charge over. Within that
sphere of authority, we have a responsibility to judge what is coming in and
going out. Is it good or is it evil? Whatever it is, we have the authority to take
dominion over our domain or sphere of influence. If it is evil, there is no

compromise to make. If it is evil, there is no time to waste. If it is evil, it is our responsibility to take action and kill it. Dead. In our tent. Done.
Go get your tent peg.

Prayer

Father, You have given me a sphere of influence. You have given me the authority to have dominion over that area. I have a responsibility before You to watch over it and take action when I see evil crouching at the door. I need wisdom to lead well. I need a passionate hatred of evil. I need Your love and Your power to rule well in every place You have given me authority. I receive what I need from You. In Jesus' name, Amen!

Activation

Invite the Holy Spirit to show you your place of leadership and influence. Who and what has He placed in your care? Ask Him to show you anything that has crept into your tent that needs to go and how to end its influence.

DAY 36: GIRL POWER—HANNAH

> But Hannah answered,
> "No, my lord, I am a woman
> troubled in spirit. I have
> drunk neither wine nor strong drink,
> but I have been pouring out my
> soul before the Lord. Do not
> regard your servant as a worthless woman,
> for all along I have been speaking out of
> my great anxiety and vexation."
> Then Eli answered, "Go in peace,
> and the God of Israel grant your petition that
> you have made to him." And she said,
> "Let your servant find favor in your eyes."
> Then the woman went her way and ate,
> and her face was no longer sad . . .
> 1 Samuel 1: 15-20

Hannah has been living with a rival in her husband's bed. This woman continuously mocks and criticizes Hannah, using the fact that she has children by him and Hannah is barren. Hannah is suffering with anxiety and extreme stress.

So, she goes to the temple and pours out her heart in prayer and petition to God. In walks Eli, the priest. He misunderstands her and calls her drunk. Wouldn't you just sink down to the pit in self-pity and have your own pity party? Not Hannah. She tells him she has been crying out to God. She doesn't even tell him what she has asked for. Eli, the priest, simply says, "Go in peace, and the God of Israel grant your petition that you have made to him."

Hannah basically says "Amen." (Amen means so be it!) Then she goes away, eats, and is happy.

Wait, what? Earlier in the text it says she is so upset and sad that she does not eat. Her husband begs her to eat and cheer up, but she doesn't. Now, when Eli, who at first accused her of being a drunk says, "God grant your petition," she eats and is happy. What is happening here?

The priests of Israel were anointed. This means the Holy Spirit was upon them. Their words, their actions, and their judgements were anointed by the Spirit and from the Lord. Hannah grabbed onto the word of the anointed one as a positive prophecy. She came into agreement with it by faith. Faith is responding with trust, agreement, and obedience to a revelation. In her heart, she said, "I have what I have asked for!"

Hannah had amazing perception and faith. She recognized, received, and believed Eli's prophetic declaration. How do we know? Because she went away and ate, and her face was no longer sad! She was able to return to her life without the anxiety and sadness. She was able to eat, sleep, and enjoy her life, knowing that her prayer had been heard and the answer was on its way. In time, Samuel, her son, was born. She had prayed for him and the Lord answered.

How different our lives would be if we took our anxieties, stress, injustices, and desires to the Lord in prayer and then recognized, received, and believed prophetic declarations with the answer to that prayer spoken in the course of conversation?

We can begin right now.

Prayer

> *Father God, You are the God who answers prayer. You say that if I ask anything in the name of Jesus, according to Your will, and do not doubt, I have what I ask for. I ask that You give me the ability to recognize when someone utters a prophetic declaration in answer to my prayers as I have conversations each day.*

Activation

What is causing you to be anxious, stressed, and tormented? Take it to the Lord today in prayer. Pour out your heart to Him. Then listen with ears to hear the prophetic declaration in the conversations you have with people of faith after praying. Grab hold of them and add faith.

DAY 37: GIRL POWER—THE WISE WOMAN

Then a wise woman called from the city,
"Listen! Listen! Tell Joab, 'Come here, that I
may speak to you.'" And he came near her, and
the woman said, "Are you Joab?" He answered,
"I am." Then she said to him, "Listen to the
words of your servant." And he answered, "I am
listening." Then she said, "They used to say in
former times, 'Let them but ask counsel at
Abel,' and so they settled a matter. I am one of
those who are peaceable and faithful in Israel.
You seek to destroy a city that is a mother in
Israel. Why will you swallow up the heritage of
the Lord?" Joab answered, "Far be it from me,
far be it, that I should swallow up or destroy!
That is not true. But a man of the hill country of
Ephraim . . . has lifted up his hand against King
David. Give up him alone, and I will withdraw
from the city." And the woman said to Joab,
"Behold, his head shall be thrown to you over
the wall." Then the woman went to all the people
in her wisdom. And they cut off the head of Sheba the
son of Bichri and threw it out to Joab. So he
blew the trumpet, and they dispersed from the
city, every man to his home."
2 Samuel 20:16-22

Conflict is inevitable. We will all face it at times. We will face it more than
once, and sometimes it will be quite serious. People get hurt in conflict, but
often much of the wounding can be avoided if we dealt with conflict wisely.

The only name given the woman in this Biblical story is "the wise woman."
What was her wisdom? She was a skilled mediator and judge in the midst of

conflict. When we examine the story, we discover her skill. She asked for the person with the authority to make decisions. She did not waste time speaking to those who had no power in the power structure. She clarified the issue. She clarified what was at stake and the interests common to both parties. She listened to the complaint, and the terms, and decided what was right and just.

Off with his head! The city was saved.

Years ago, when I was brand-new to pastoral leadership, the lead pastor fell in adultery. I was shocked, stunned, disappointed, and felt betrayed. The entire leadership team was wounded and confused. Suddenly, things grew even worse. People were competing for power and betraying one another over the smallest issues. Gossip and suspicion were everywhere. I became offended, angry, and wounded. The leaders over me were treating me unfairly and I reacted with whining and self-pity. They soon decided they could not trust me as a leader on the team and I was asked to step down from my position. I was so hurt. It was a painful time.

God healed my wounds. When He did, He spoke very clearly to me. He told me that though I had been treated unfairly and misunderstood, I had played a part in my own demise. He showed me that I had given into my emotions and allowed them to lead me. He gave me a little phrase to live by from that point on. He said, "Do not react in emotion, but respond in wisdom."

I have lived by that principle ever since. My emotions do not lead me or make the decisions in my life. I take the time to deal with my emotions so that wisdom can lead me in making decisions in any and every circumstance. I am slow to react, but when I make a decision, it is decisive. These days, I am known to be a wise woman.

The wise woman of 2 Samuel 20 did not give into emotionality. She asked questions, listened to the answers, and made right judgments. She did not entertain gossip. She did not give in to grumbling or complaining. She did not scream and yell, weep and beg, or manipulate or seduce. She responded in wisdom. She was a wise woman.

Prayer

Father, I want to be a wise woman. I want to make wise decisions so that those around me and those following me are safe and prosperous. Give me a sound mind to make sound judgments. In Jesus' name, Amen.

Activation

Invite the Holy Spirit to show you any place in your life where your emotions are leading you, rather than wisdom. Take some time to thank God for emotions and seek His wisdom for how to deal with them. Then, invite the Holy Spirit to show you the way of wisdom in any place in your life where there is conflict. Ask Him the wisest way to deal with it.

☐ Who is the person we should speak to?
☐ What questions need to be asked?
☐ How do we clarify the real issue?
☐ What is the common ground or interest?
☐ What is the best solution that will cause the least harm to innocent parties?

DAY 38: GIRL POWER—RAHAB

And Joshua the son of Nun sent two men
secretly from Shittim as spies, saying, "Go,
view the land, especially Jericho." And they
went and came into the house of a prostitute
whose name was Rahab and lodged there.
Joshua 2:1

The book of the genealogy of Jesus Christ, the
son of David, the son of Abraham. Abraham
was the father of Isaac, and Isaac the father of
Jacob, and Jacob the father of Judah and his
brothers, and Judah the father of Perez and
Zerah by Tamar, and Perez the father of Hezron,
and Hezron the father of Ram, and Ram the
father of Amminadab, and Amminadab the
father of Nahshon, and Nahshon the father of
Salmon, and Salmon the father of Boaz by
Rahab . . .
Matthew 1:1-4 (emphasis mine)

In Matthew, we read the names of those in the family line of Jesus. Only a few women are named, one of whom is Rahab. Rahab was a prostitute in the city of Jericho—the city whose walls fell down flat at the shout of Joshua and his people. The city whose destruction was complete annihilation—except for Rahab the prostitute and her family.

Rahab was the most unlikely hero. Her gender made her unlikely. Her Canaanite ethnicity made her unlikely. Her profession made her unlikely. Yet, it is Rahab we meet on the eve of the great conquest of the Promised Land. She lives on the walls of the city. In many ways, she lives a double life. In her city, among her people, she was outcast, but not outlawed. She was dishonored but accepted. Yet, the writer of Hebrews remembers her in the famous chapter of faith as a woman of faith who saved her family and was instrumental in bringing down Jericho. James remembers Rahab as a model of faith accompanied by works for saving the spies in Jericho.

The spies of Israel and soldiers of Jericho both come to the prostitute's door. Doors in prophetic language represent passageways or opportunities. They open or close the way to the next place. Standing at the door, Rahab seizes her opportunity for a new life. She would no longer be a person things happen to—she would now be a person that makes things happen.

When she tells the spies the whole city is seized with fear because of their God, sends the soldiers in the wrong direction, opposes the command of her king, and rescues the spies, she breaks through the boundaries of her present life and crosses an invisible line to place both feet in a new life of faith. She leaves everything behind in that moment—her religion, her community, her hometown, her business, and her way of life.

She saw her divine opportunity, and left everything to take it. In the Gospels, when Jesus calls the disciples, they immediately leave everything to follow Him. Rahab responded in faith to the call of God, and God remembers her as a woman of faith. Her past is wiped away. Her future was included in the line of Christ.

Rahab is a hero of faith.

Prayer

> *Father, Rahab seized her opportunity to follow You and started a new life. She became a hero of the faith. I want to know when opportunity comes to my door in any form. I want to seize the opportunity for a life of faith. I choose to follow You now, wherever You take me, wherever it leads. I choose a life of faith. In Jesus' name, Amen.*

Activation

Reflect over your life. Invite the Holy Spirit to show you where you have the opportunity to seize something new, something powerful, something faithful. Write what He shows you and decide what you will choose.

Are there things in your past you fear are held against you? Do you live with one foot in the past and one foot in the present, but close your eyes to the future? Are you ready to make a decision to put both feet into the life of faith and leave the rest behind? Talk to the Lord about it today.

DAY 39: GIRL POWER—RUTH, PART I

Then she arose with her daughters-in-law to
return from the country of Moab, for she heard
in the fields of Moab that the Lord had visited
his people and given them food.
Ruth 1:6

Ruth, her mother-in-law Naomi, and her sister-in-law Orpah, have lost everything. Their husbands have died. They have no children. They are in a foreign land in the middle of a famine. They hear a story about Bethlehem. God has visited His people. He has given them bread. The three women must decide how they will respond.

Naomi is going home. Orpah turns back, forfeiting a future with God for the safe and familiar. Ruth turns toward the future and gives her life into God's hands.

Ruth risks starting over.

A bitter end is where a new journey can begin. God is the God of new beginnings. There are times in our lives when we will have to allow for a new vision. We cannot keep doing the same thing over and over and expect different results! We may have to stop investing time or money on something that has stopped producing fruit and is no longer viable. We may have to step away from unhealthy relationships, old ways of doing things, addictive cycles, or abusive circumstances.

We will have to resist the temptation to stay where things are safe and familiar. We will have to stop listening to a voice of bitterness that says there is no use in looking for a better life. We will have to listen to the voice of God, decide to start over, and go where there is bread. Going where there is bread means to go where God is present and presently working.

At the end of Ruth 1, she and Naomi arrived in Bethlehem at the time of the *barley* harvest. Barley harvest was the time of the Passover—a time of release and deliverance from death and its effects. It was a sign of the covenant faithfulness of God to bring abundance and blessing and *redemption*. It was a sign pointing to the future. The barley harvest would one day coincide with Pentecost, the time of the new covenant and the pouring out of the Holy Spirit on God's people, the time of a powerful, fresh empowerment.

Prayer

> *Father, I want to go where there is bread. Wherever there are areas in my life that are dead and not bearing fruit, help me to start over and go on a new journey. Wherever I have listened to a voice of reason that tells me not to risk it, or a voice of bitterness that tells me I have no future and nothing will ever change, forgive me. I come out of agreement with them today. Where a sense of loss has kept me depressed and unable to move forward, or worse, has turned me backwards, Father, in Your loving kindness, speak to my heart and heal me. Reveal where You are working and point me in the right direction. Send a barley harvest into my life! In Jesus' name, Amen.*

Activation

Is it time to start over in any area of your life? What has held you back? Is there any area in your life where you have traded in the promises of God for what is safe and familiar?

- ☐ Invite the Holy Spirit to speak to you about where God is present and presently moving around you.
- ☐ Decide if you will start over.
- ☐ Go where there is bread!

DAY 40: GIRL POWER—REBEKAH

And he said, "O Lord, God of my master
Abraham, please grant me
success today and show steadfast
love to my master Abraham. Behold, I am
standing by the spring of water,
and the daughters of the men of the
city are coming out to draw water.
Let the young woman to whom I shall say,
'Please let down your jar that I may
drink,' and who shall say, 'Drink,
and I will water your camels'—let
her be the one whom you have appointed
for your servant Isaac.
By this I shall know that you have shown
steadfast love to my master." Before he
had finished speaking, behold,
Rebekah . . . came out with
her water jar on her shoulder.
Genesis 24:12-15

"Before they call I will answer;
while they are yet speaking I will hear."
Isaiah 65:24

Abraham was old and about to die. His wife Sarah had already passed on. He had a son, Isaac, who was not yet married. Abraham had been faithful to God all of his life. Isaac was the son God promised Abraham and Sarah. He was the fulfillment of a prophetic promise and came by a divinely appointed miracle. He couldn't have just any wife. She needed to be very special.

Abraham appoints his servant to this very important task. He makes the servant swear an oath that he will take a wife only from a select group of people. He will have to travel a long way to find them and find this very special girl. The servant is fearful. What if he cannot fulfill the task? Abraham prophesies that an Angel of the Lord will go before him and he will have divine help for the task.

In spite of all the unknowns, the servant goes on this special journey. We are all in suspense. He is going to a place he has not been, to a people he has never met, to find a girl whose identity is completely unknown by him or Abraham. Yet, he is charged to somehow find this very special girl for this miracle man of promise. He is anxious.

He has served in Abraham's household long enough to understand there is a God who has been faithful to Abraham. He has served in Abraham's household long enough to have seen Abraham talk in prayer to this God. So, he prays to Abraham's God.

And before he is finished speaking, God sends the answer—a very special girl named Rebekah. She is the answer to his prayers.

People all over the world today are praying. We are the answer to someone's prayer today. What a special privilege.

Prayer

> *Father, You are listening to the prayers of millions of people all over the world right now. You are the God who answers even before we are finished speaking. You often send the answer in the form of a person, flesh and blood to represent You, to bring the good news, to comfort the brokenhearted and to set the captive free. I want to be the answer to someone's prayer. Open my eyes to see the opportunity when it is in front of me, when I am the answer You are sending. Give me a willing and joyful heart to say "Yes." In Jesus' name, Amen.*

Activation

When was the last time you were aware that you were the answer God sent to someone's prayer? How did it happen? How did you respond? What was the result? How do you think you might be the answer to someone's prayer today or in this season of your life? How will you respond? What might the outcome be because you responded with the understanding that God was sending you in answer to a prayer?

———————————⟨◇⟩———————————

DAY 41: GIRL POWER—
THE WIDOW OF ZAREPHATH

Then the word of the Lord came to him, "Arise,
go to Zarephath, which belongs to Sidon, and
dwell there. Behold, I have commanded a
widow there to feed you." So he arose and went
to Zarephath. And when he came to the gate of
the city, behold, a widow was there gathering
sticks. And he called to her and said, "Bring me
a little water in a vessel, that I may drink." And
as she was going to bring it, he called to her and
said, "Bring me a morsel of bread in your
hand." And she said, "As the Lord your God
lives, I have nothing baked, only a handful of
flour in a jar and a little oil in a jug. And now I
am gathering a couple of sticks that I may go in
and prepare it for myself and my son, that we
may eat it and die." And Elijah said to her, "Do
not fear; go and do as you have said. But first
make me a little cake of it and bring it to me,
and afterward make something for yourself and
your son. For thus says the Lord, the God of
Israel, 'The jar of flour shall not be spent, and
the jug of oil shall not be empty, until the day
that the Lord sends rain upon the earth.'"
1 Kings 17:8-14

And she went and did as Elijah said...The jar of
flour was not spent, neither did the jug of oil
become empty, according to the word of the
Lord that he spoke by Elijah.
1 Kings 17:15-16

The widow of Zaraphath has lost everything and is about to give in to death.
She cannot see past her present circumstances. The prophet Elijah shows up

on her doorstep expecting her to feed him. He has a word of the Lord. God said He arranged for this widow to provide for him. Apparently, she didn't get the memo. When Elijah asks for bread, her fears and expectations are revealed. There is not enough—there is no future. Elijah prophesies to her that God will provide for her. There is a future for her and her son. He also tells her to make him a little cake first.

The widow will have to face her fear of lack. She will have to change her perspective by taking her eyes off what is, and see what can be. She will have to see beyond her present circumstances. She will also have to act on the word of the prophet before she sees the miracle of provision.

It is when she acts on the word, in spite of her own need, that the miracle happens. It is when she acts on the word, in spite of her fear, that the miracle happens. It is when she acts on the word, in spite of what she sees with her natural eyes, that the miracle happens. It is when she acts on the word, which reveals faith, that the miracle comes to pass.

I believe the Lord wants to break off a fear of lack in our lives. So many of us have lived in poverty, never feeling like there is enough money, time, energy, food, or love—whatever it is. We feel like the widow. There is barely enough for today, and not enough for tomorrow. When we believe this, we think like a widow and act like a widow.

But we are *not* widows. We are brides with the most powerful Husband in all the universe. It is time we began looking beyond our present circumstances, believed the Scriptures about provision, and acted on them. When we act on what is true, the miracle begins. Today is the day to receive your provision. Today is the day to say no to lack, break up with poverty thinking and receive hope.

Prayer

> *Father, Jesus said He came to give me an abundant life. You are the God who provides all I need, backs me up, and hears me when I call. Today Lord, right now, I invite You to change the way I think and remove every habit of thought that partners with a spirit of fear, a spirit of lack, a poverty mindset, or a widow's mindset. Set me free. I come out of agreement with*

lack, fear, poverty, and widowhood. I am the bride of Christ.
My husband is Christ Himself and He loves me, provides for
me, protects me, and supplies all my needs out of His rich
abundance. I receive it right now. In Jesus' name, Amen.

Activation

☐ Invite the Holy Spirit to stir up your faith.
☐ Make a list of your needs. Be sure to include needs that are not financial—time, energy, healing, etc.
☐ Over each need declare:

> "For thus says the Lord, the God of _____ (Insert your own name), '*My* jar of flour will not be spent, and my jug of oil shall not be empty, until the day that the Lord sends rain upon the earth and my season is changed."

☐ Declare that God will provide for each of the listed needs, just as He did for the widow of Zarephath!
☐ Joyfully thank the Lord that He is your provider and that provision for every need is on its way.

◈

DAY 42: GIRL POWER—THE WIDOW AND ELISHA

> Elisha said . . . "Tell me; what have you in the
> house?" And she said, "Your servant has
> nothing in the house except a jar of oil." Then
> he said, "Go outside, borrow vessels from all
> your neighbors, empty vessels and not too few.
> Then go in and shut the door behind yourself
> and your sons and pour into all these vessels.
> And when one is full, set it aside."
> 2 Kings 4:2-4

I have been to hundreds of conferences all over the world. People often come to me and ask, "Do you have a word for me?" Over the years, I have encountered many who go from conference to conference asking for a prophetic word. They want God to do something miraculous in their lives. They want to be used by God. They want to see their lives fulfill the purposes for which they were created. It seems to never happen. Why? The answer is often that they haven't done anything with the prophecies, gifts, and call they have.

Elisha asked the widow what she already had. She answered that she had nothing but a jar of oil. It seemed like nothing, but it was the place to begin.

If we want to see God do the miraculous in our lives, we have to start with the word we have already received. The one jar of oil. We have to be bold about acting on it. The widow's oil would go as far as her boldness would go.

The word Elisha gave her was about miracle provision and multiplication of her "oil." It was what she already had in her hand. In order to receive the fulfillment of the prophecy regarding the miracle, she would have to take actions—go, borrow, pour.

Interestingly, oil in prophetic symbolism can mean the Holy Spirit's anointing. Want your anointing to be multiplied? Do you want to see the prophetic words over your life come to pass? Act on them!

What's in your hand? This is the place to begin. When you have boldly acted on it, He will give you more, and He will give you the next step. He will even give you the next prophecy you need.

Prayer

> *Father, I give You what is in my hand. Whatever skill, talent, gift, anointing, prophecy, calling, or purpose that is in my life—use it, multiply it, and pour it out. In Jesus' name, Amen.*

Activation

Invite the Holy Spirit to bring to your mind every prophecy you have ever been given. Are there any you have not acted on? Ask Him to speak to you about what action to take and then do it.

Invite the Holy Spirit to show you what is in your house (calling) and hand (talent, gift, skill). Ask Him how and where to begin using it. Then go!

DAY 43: GIRL POWER—TAMAR

> About three months later Judah was told,
> "Tamar your daughter-in-law has been immoral.
> Moreover, she is pregnant by immorality. . ." As
> she was being brought out, she sent word to her
> father-in-law, "By the man to whom these
> belong, I am pregnant." And she said, "Please
> identify whose these are, the signet and the cord
> and the staff." Then Judah identified them and
> said, "She is more righteous than I . . ."
> Genesis 38:24-26

> The book of the genealogy of Jesus Christ, the
> son of David, the son of Abraham. Abraham
> was the father of Isaac, and Isaac the father of
> Jacob, and Jacob the father of Judah and his
> brothers, and Judah the father of Perez and
> Zerah by Tamar . . .
> Matthew 1:1-3

Tamar is the only female in the Old Testament who is called "righteous." You would never guess it by reading her story! Tamar poses as a prostitute to trick her father-in-law and become pregnant with his child. When she is found to be pregnant, she is accused of being immoral and is taken out to be burned alive.

But she is not the one who has been unfaithful. It is those around her. She has been treated unfairly, condemned as cursed, and rejected. She was not unmarried; she was a widow. According to the customs, she was right in enacting the levirate law. This law says when a Hebrew man died without children, his widow was to be given to the nearest kinsman to produce offspring to preserve the family line. This had not been done for her because they wrongfully blamed her for the death of her husband. She was misunderstood and maligned. Worse yet, she was told to go home and wait. They would come for her in time. But that time never came.

Her unwillingness to be a victim or take offense, and her willingness to break away from the limits placed on her by others, not only exonerate her, but preserve the prophetic promises of God in the family line. She is called righteous by those who condemned her, and honored by her name being included in the genealogy of Jesus.

Sometimes we give up too soon. Sometimes we allow ourselves to continue to be victimized. Sometimes we conform to the criticisms and misguided thinking of others. Tamar refused to shut up, sit down, and go home. She did what was right in the eyes of God, even though others did not understand.

That's girl power!

Prayer

> *Father, I refuse to be a victim. I refuse to quit and go backwards. I will not take offense, but I will also not be limited by other people's thoughts about me. I will walk by Your Spirit and fulfill the call on my life.*

Activation

Invite the Holy Spirit to speak to you about the limits, criticisms, and rejections you have lived under. How have they restricted you? In what ways have you conformed? Invite the Holy Spirit to show you how to move out from under those things and continue in the call on your life.

DAY 44: GIRL POWER—PHILIP'S DAUGHTERS

On the next day we departed and came to
Caesarea, and we entered the house of Philip the
evangelist, who was one of the seven, and
stayed with him. He had four unmarried
daughters, who prophesied.
Acts 21:8-9

And in the last days it shall be, God declares,
that I will pour out my Spirit on all flesh,
and your sons and your daughters shall
prophesy, and your young men shall see visions,
and your old men shall dream dreams;
even on my male servants and female servants
in those days I will pour out my Spirit,
and they shall prophesy.
Acts 2:17-18

Phillip, who was a part of the early charismatic revival, had four daughters who prophesied. Phillip is described as an evangelist. His daughters are described as prophetic ministers. The gifts of the Holy Spirit are given to male and female. Our gender does not limit what the Lord can call us to or gift us for. Paul tells us the gifts of the Spirit are distributed according to His will. In the entire chapter of 1 Corinthians 12, where Paul discusses the gifts of the Spirit being sourced and distributed by the Holy Spirit, he never mentions gender.

Growing up, my family attended a little church in the neighborhood. We were taught that women could do many things in the church, except preach, teach, and prophesy. When I had an encounter with the Holy Spirit and God called me to full-time ministry, I was worried. He was asking me to preach, teach, and prophesy, but I wasn't sure this was okay.

So I studied. Here is what I found.

- [ ] Jesus included women in His life and ministry as a model or witness to the early church of how the new covenant restores male and female to ministry.
- [ ] Jesus did not prohibit women from receiving empowerment for witness. There were 120 in the upper room waiting according to Jesus' directive, which included the apostles, the women with them, his mother, and brothers.
- [ ] All the prophetic promises regarding the new covenant and the outpouring of the Spirit are inclusive of women (Acts 2, Joel 2:28-29, Isaiah 59:19-21, Numbers 11:29).
- [ ] In the Book of Acts, by the time we come to Stephen, women are being recognized as leaders and influencers in the church and considered as dangerous as the men worthy of persecution. Saul would drag *both* off to prison.
- [ ] In the New Testament, women were house church leaders (house churches were the only kind of church at that time).
- [ ] In Romans 16, Paul calls a woman, Junia, an outstanding apostle, Phoebe a "servant" or deacon and leader of a house church, and Priscilla the teacher of Apollos and a fellow worker—a term used for other male leaders.
- [ ] Paul included and affirmed women in the ministry of the kingdom. He made no distinction between the roles of male and female in leadership.
- [ ] In 1 Corinthians 14:34-35, Paul is instructing the church in how to go about allowing the women to learn, how to dress when giving public address, and how to maintain order while they were learning. He was not forbidding women from leading and speaking.
- [ ] 1 Timothy 2:11-15, Paul is admonishing both men and women to dress appropriately, and allowing women to study and learn in silence—in full submission to God and their teachers. He is wanting to set the order for Jesus followers that avoids the model of the cult in their city in which women rule over men, yet at the same time not making men superior. Women are not to take over leadership and solely dominate the church; they are to develop the gifts and call on their lives alongside their brothers.

All God's people, male and female, are all called to good works as in Ephesians 2:10 and John 10:32. Everyone has a part to play in the drama of the kingdom. What is your part?

Prayer

Father, You created me female and it is beautiful and powerful. Fill me with Your Holy Spirit and activate the gifts in my life. Send me to advance the kingdom and do "good works," which are miraculous. I will do whatever You call me to do. In Jesus' name, Amen.

Activation

Take some time to think through your understanding of a woman's role in ministry or kingdom service. How has this impacted your understanding of your own role in the body of Christ? Spend some time journaling about your heart's desire for ministry.

Invite the Holy Spirit to speak to you about your part in the kingdom and the church. Write down what you hear. Invite the Holy Spirit to show you your next steps to doing "good works."

DAY 45: GIRL POWER—RUTH, PART II

And Ruth the Moabite said to Naomi,
"Let me go to the field and glean among the
ears of grain after him in whose sight I shall
find favor."
Ruth 2:2

Ruth is bold. She goes out to find favor.

Where we find favor, we find our field. In our field of favor, we are recognized for who we are and the gifts we possess. When we find favor, we find the right relationships and resources to fulfill our calling. When we find favor, we find the blessing of support for advancement, protection, and unusual blessing.

- Favor brings resource and special provision.
- Favor opens doors of unprecedented opportunity.
- Favor brings influence and influential networks.
- Favor releases unsolicited blessing and advancement.
- Favor brings divine connection and partnership for expansion and projects.
- Favor brings protection and support.
- Favor promotes in position and power.

Favor comes from God and men.

Ruth finds favor in the field of the kinsman redeemer. Ruth didn't need to know what field to go to. She was directed by God's sovereignty because He favored her. When she came into her field of favor, she found favor with all those in the field with her. When she found favor, she received recognition, promotion, provision, protection, and more favor. She used her favor to bless Naomi, which won her even more favor. In time, she received a complete restoration of all that had been lost in the former season—first for Naomi and then for herself.

When restoration came, revival burst forth in the form of a new life.

We are about to experience historic geopolitical, economic, religious, and cultural change. This change is setting us up for revival. God is about to move in this time among those you would least expect. Ruth was the person we least expect to usher in a revival, but she does. A little favor goes a long way.

Are you ready? Let's go out and find our favor!

Prayer

> *Father, I want to grow in favor with You and others. I want to be an instrument of restoration and revival in the lives of others. I want to see Your kingdom come on earth as it is in heaven. Move me into the field of my favor as I continue to walk faithfully with You. In Jesus' name, Amen.*

Activation

Find Your Favor Personal Inventory

Why find your favor? Because it will show you the places where God is inviting you to seize the opportunity before you.

CAUTION. Tools are not rules. There are times when we will experience opposition because we are in the right place, but this is not a sign of disfavor. Discernment is key here. Invite the Holy Spirit to guide you.

- ☐ What is in your hand right now?
- ☐ What issue or situation is breaking your heart right now?
- ☐ List all the places where you are giving, serving, working, training, showing up, and involved.

In the context of those places listed:

- ☐ Where does it seem evident that God is moving?
- ☐ Where does it feel effortless—like you were "born for this" and it fills rather than drains you?

- Where do you gain positive attention from others—approval, support, and vigorous encouragement from those around you?
- Where are you being invited more and more to use your expertise, natural talent, and gifting from God?
- Where are you finding that you are being promoted and given "special" privileges?
- Where are you finding that you are "protected"?
- Where are you being given resource and provision? (money, people, network, strategy, etc.)
- Where are you finding and recognizing favor?
- In the area where you recognize you have favor, what is a next step you could take if you were ten times bolder and knew the answer would be yes?
- Are you willing to take the risk?
- What will it look like—what is the plan or strategy for taking that next step?
- When will you take the risk?

Now invite the Holy Spirit to speak to you about where your field of favor is and what you are to be doing.

———————————————⟨◇⟩———————————————

"Many women have done excellently, but you
surpass them all. Charm is deceitful, and beauty is vain,
but a woman who fears the Lord is to be praised. Give
her of the fruit of her hands, and let her works
praise her in the gates."
Proverbs 31:29-31

Proverbs 31. Countless times I sat low in my chair in church, squirming in my seat, listening to a painful message taken from Proverbs 31 on Mother's Day. Some young preacher, who did not know what it was like to be a mom, would go line by line through the text, measuring the worth of all the women in the room. None of us measured up. Most of us felt put to shame. On and on he would talk about the things we should be doing if we wanted to be praised and adored. In those days, I certainly did not look forward to Mother's Day in church!

This is not the purpose behind Proverbs 31. It is a beautiful poem written by the queen mother to her son, who would be king. It is her advice regarding the kind of woman the king should be looking for. It is a picture of a woman who is thriving by being all she can be. Her family is thriving because she is being everything she is called to be. She isn't limited because she has a family; she is praised for it. She isn't hindered by her gender; she is honored.

Interestingly, Jewish women love Proverbs 31. They recite it to girlfriends as a way of saying, "You are doing a great job! Keep going!" Why? They look at Proverbs 31 as permission from God to do anything and everything God calls them to do—business, education, family, leadership, and even handling money.

You have permission to be everything God has dreamed for you to be. You have permission to celebrate being a woman. You have permission to enjoy your life as a woman.

What is the true measure of a woman? The fear of the Lord. It isn't whether you are married or single, a business executive or a stay-at-home mother. The measure of a woman is not anything to do with your roles, your success or failures, the size of your family, or the size of your bank account. It has to do with your heart.

If your heart belongs to the Lord, you are a Proverbs 31 woman.

Prayer

> *Father, thank You! You tell me, "You can do it! Keep going!" You give me permission to be everything You dream of. You love that I am a woman. Thank You. In Jesus' name, Amen.*

Activation
Read Proverbs 31:10-31. Invite the Holy Spirit to show you how free you are in the eyes of the Lord. Ask Him which verses He wants to bring alive in a brand-new way in your life. Journal about it and pray it into your life.

Think about the women you love. Invite the Holy Spirit to show you how you can use this passage to encourage them today. Which verses does God want to use to give them permission and freedom? Write out the encouragement in a card and send it.

DAY 47: GIRL POWER—JOCHEBED

"This is one of the Hebrews' children." Then his
sister said to Pharaoh's daughter, "Shall I go
and call you a nurse from the Hebrew women to
nurse the child for you?" And Pharaoh's
daughter said to her, "Go." So the girl went and
called the child's mother. And Pharaoh's
daughter said to her, "Take this child away and
nurse him for me, and I will give you your
wages." So the woman took the child and
nursed him. When the child grew older, she
brought him to Pharaoh's daughter, and he
became her son.
Exodus 2:6-10

Jochebed has given birth to Moses, the promised deliverer for the enslaved nation of Israel. Pharaoh has ordered that all male children be killed. Jochebed has no power or influence to change her situation. The life of her son hangs in the balance. She has hidden Moses three months, until she could hide him no more. She builds a boat and sets him afloat. She lets go.

It is an incredible story of how Moses was raised up as the deliverer of His people. I marvel at this woman. I wonder, are any of us secure enough in our identity and humble enough to serve when we thought we would lead? Are we able to let go of something we birthed and allow someone else to raise it up? Do we trust God enough to lead from obscurity so that God's will can be done?

Jochebed was Moses' mother. Yet, in order to save him, she had to let him go. She became his servant, a wet nurse, while someone else became his mother. We know God had a purpose and brought this turn of events about so that Moses would receive the finest education and understanding of the Egyptian culture. Having Pharaoh's daughter as a mother ensured he would be protected from harm.

Jochebed could not have known any of that when she let go of his little reed boat. She is incredible! It takes a self-sacrificing love and humility to put God's sometimes mysterious purposes before our own needs and desires. Sometimes God will ask us to lead from underneath or from the back. Sometimes God will ask us to support someone else, even though we could do a better job. Sometimes we won't know why.

If we will risk letting go if these circumstances, we will be positioned to influence leaders and give birth to deliverance for many others.

Prayer

Father, You have purposes greater than my vision. Secure me in Your love. Deliver me from pride and selfish ambition and anything that would keep me from being able to serve in the position of influence, whether it be above or below. Give me a love and a faith big enough to not need title or position. In Jesus' name, Amen.

Activation

Sit in the presence of the Holy Spirit and answer these questions:

- Am I secure enough in my identity and humble enough to serve when I thought I would lead?
- Am I able to let go of something I birthed and allow someone else to raise it up?
- Do I trust God enough to lead from obscurity so that His ultimate will can be done?

DAY 48: GIRL POWER—MIRIAM

Then Miriam the prophetess,
the sister of Aaron, took a
tambourine in her hand,
and all the women went
out after her with tambourines
and dancing.
And Miriam sang to them:
"Sing to the Lord,
for he has triumphed gloriously;
the horse and his rider he has
thrown into the sea."
Exodus 15:20-21

Miriam is the first female prophet in Scripture. She was a leader alongside Moses and Aaron in the greatest deliverance of the Old Testament. In this passage of Scripture she leads the women in worship with a prophetic song. It is the first women's ministry meeting!

I have a confession to make. I have never liked women's ministry. I know. It's a shock. But let me explain. There was a time when I was going to a very large church. Sundays were marvelous, and so I thought the women's ministry meeting would be too. I looked forward to going. I made my plans and attended a meeting. There were hundreds of women in the room. How exciting! When the speaker started, the topic was how to keep an organized home.

I am prophetic. One of the ways I receive revelation from God is feeling. I feel emotion in a room or simply know in my understanding what people in a room are experiencing. I could feel grief, loss, sadness, and bondage. It was very uncomfortable. I thought for sure that after the topic, there would be a ministry time for the women in the room. They needed God. I was wrong. The entire night encouraged women to keep a nice clean home for their families, but never addressed their personal needs, or God's hopes and dreams for them.

Not all women's meetings are like this, especially in the days we are living in. Women are being challenged, given vision, and empowered. It is very exciting.

I can imagine the women's meeting Miriam led on the other side of the Red Sea, with the pillar of cloud, God's presence, hovering above, Pharaoh's army newly defeated behind, and the Promised Land beckoning ahead. Miriam, the prophet, prophesied and led hundreds and thousands of women just delivered from their bondage in a song about the glory of God. Can you hear them singing? Can you hear the pounding of their feet in the dance?

I'm telling you the truth, this is the kind of women's ministry—no, women's *movement*—God is looking for! This is the kind of women's movement women are looking for!

Prayer

> *Father, I want to be a part of the women's movement You are bringing. I want to bring You glory. In the name of Jesus, I pray that women leaders everywhere would receive a fresh passion and vision for a women's movement that glorifies God. I ask, Father God, that You would raise up women all over the world to join together in the song of victory over the enemy and that worship would rise up from among them. Give us a kingdom movement, a God movement, a revival movement. Give us the kind of women's movement that our daughters and granddaughters will hunger to be a part of. Give us a women's movement that births revival, evangelism, mission, social justice, and every kind of kingdom work and miracle! We want it, Lord! Bring Your presence, Your Word, Your power, and Your love. Raise up Your women! In Jesus' name, Amen!*

Activation

Go back to Day 9 and read your activation response. Write out a prayer declaration, based on your response to Day 9, expanding it to include all women in your nation. Declare it out loud over yourself and your nation in prayer. Ask God to bring it to pass!

DAY 49: GIRL POWER—LYDIA

And on the Sabbath day… we sat down and
spoke to the women who had come together.
One who heard us was a woman named Lydia,
from the city of Thyatira, a seller of purple
goods, who was a worshiper of God. The Lord
opened her heart to pay attention to what was
said by Paul. And after she was baptized, and
her household as well, she urged us, saying, "If
you have judged me to be faithful to the Lord,
come to my house and stay."
Acts 16:13-15

Lydia was a wealthy business woman. God moved on her heart to listen, hear, and act on what Paul said. She was baptized, influenced her entire household so they also believed and were baptized, and then opened a house church. We don't know if she gave up her business, but we do know that she became a house church leader when she encountered God.

A few weeks ago, I received a phone call from a friend. This friend wanted to introduce me to a young man who was feeling compelled by God to lay hands on the sick. Because I minister in healing with an organization called Apostolic Network of Global Awakening often, this friend thought I was the right person to speak with this young man. I agreed to meet them.

The young man turned out to be a famous young man in the arts and entertainment field. When we spoke, he began to tell me about an encounter he had with Jesus and began to weep. He said he is overwhelmed by the love and compassion of Jesus for people. When he walks by people, he can feel their illnesses or their bondage. He has started to pray for people for healing and deliverance everywhere he goes. When he is home, he walks down to the coffee shop to find people he can pray for. He is seeing miracles. Yet, he doesn't know anyone who is feeling the way he does, doing these things, or believing God does miracles today. Could I help him? Yes. I can help. I can help him understand God's ways and help him understand the call of God on his life. I can help him deal with the great changes coming, because I have been through them myself.

I believe many are about to encounter the Lord in a way that changes their lives and vocation. We may be the Paul who sits down, speaks to those gathered, and leads a Lydia to the Lord. We may be the friend to whom someone can reach out to help explain the miraculous ways of God and help them into their new calling. We may be the Lydia who encounters the Lord and whose life gets radically changed.

At different times, we will experience all three.

Prayer

> *Father God, there are people everywhere in my neighborhood, city, and nation who are ripe for an encounter with You. Come, Holy Spirit! Touch their hearts and minds, bring salvation, and the baptism of the Holy Spirit to their lives. Compel them into the kingdom of light and send them to do kingdom business. Start a revival movement full of business owners, government leaders, famous people, musicians, doctors, and millionaires. Touch the politicians and the university professors, and all those in positions of influence and power. Touch the smallest and the largest, the youngest and the oldest, men and women. In Jesus' name, Amen!*

Activation

Invite the Holy Spirit to give you the names or show you the faces of three powerful, wealthy, or famous people in your nation to pray for. Ask Him to show you why He chose these particular people. For example, what would their encounter with the Lord affect in the nation? Ask Him to give you a prayer strategy or plan for how to pray for them. Ask Him how long He would have you pray for them—days, weeks, or months.

DAY 50: GIRL POWER—
THE SHUNAMMITE WOMAN

One day Elisha went on to Shunem,
where a wealthy woman lived, who
urged him to eat some food. So
whenever he passed that way,
he would turn in there to eat food.
And she said to her husband,
"Behold now, I know that this
is a holy man of God who is
continually passing our way.
Let us make a small room on
the roof with walls and put
there for him a bed, a table,
a chair, and a lamp, so that
whenever he comes to us,
he can go in there."
2 Kings 4:8-10

Today I want you to reflect and invite the Holy Spirit to show you a holy man or woman that is passing through your life right now that you are called to be a Shunammite for. This may be a gift and calling for the rest of your life, or a season as you learn to bless and serve another leader. We all will be a Shunammite to someone at some time. It is a powerful blessing from the Lord to serve in this way.

Let me tell you a story from my own life when someone was a Shunammite for me.

It was a very intense time in my life. I was a wife, mother, and grandmother. I was a full-time pastor in a church and a full-time doctoral student writing a doctoral thesis. My husband worked full-time as a battalion chief in the fire department, which meant he was often away several days at a time. My precious mother had been diagnosed with ovarian cancer, which meant I was serving my extended family during this time as well. In addition to this, as if it were not enough, I suffered from migraine headaches and chronic pain. I was struggling to write my thesis, because if I spent time writing I would have a migraine triggered by back spasms. I was falling way behind.

Then one day, a migraine came and put me in the hospital for a whole week. Afterwards, I was incredibly weak and in constant pain.

A friend heard what happened and called. She said she wanted to bless me with what was in her hand because she felt the Lord saying what I was writing was important for the kingdom. She was a massage therapist. She came to my house every week for three months and gave me a 60-90-minute, deep-tissue massage for no fee.

The migraines went away almost completely during that time. I finished my doctoral thesis on time.

To this day, I cannot express enough gratitude for the gift of a Shunammite in my own life and ministry. I have known other ministers who have been blessed in many ways by the rest and rescue provided them through a Shunammite. Sometimes, the provision allows for expanding the ministry, sometimes it allows for the expanding of time and energy, sometimes it allows for rest and being renewed.

It is always the kind of blessing that bears fruit in the kingdom, and honors God through the honoring of His servants.

Prayer

Father, You have blessed me to be a blessing. I want to be a Shunammite woman who blesses Your servants as they serve You. Bless me with even greater blessing so that I can bless them. If there is a holy man or woman You have brought into my life that is a divine appointment for me to bring blessing to, show me. In Jesus' name, Amen.

Activation

Reflect on those in your life right now who are serving the Lord full-time. Ask the Lord how you might bless them today. Invite the Holy Spirit to speak to you about being an ongoing blessing to them.

DAY 51: GIRL POWER—EVE

Then the Lord God said, "It is not good that the
man should be alone; I will make him a helper
fit for him."
Genesis 2:18

So the Lord God caused a deep sleep to fall
upon the man, and while he slept took one of his
ribs and closed up its place with flesh. And the
rib that the Lord God had taken from the man he
made into a woman and brought her to the man.
Genesis 2:21-22

Eve was created to be a helper fit for Adam. Perfectly fit. The Lord saw that Adam was alone and it was not good. So, God created Eve. The Hebrew word for "helper" is actually two words. One of the words, *eser,* means "rescuer, strength, warrior." The word is used twenty-one times in the Old Testament, and it is usually referring to God. By connecting and using the other word, *kenegdo,* with the word *eser,* Genesis 2:18 is intended to be read, "I will make a power or strength equal and corresponding to man." In other words, God created two powers who were one. They were equally made in God's image. They were both strong and powerful. They were fit to partner in the work of God together.

When Adam and Eve fell in sin, their partnership was damaged. They were to partner together to take dominion over the earth, but now they fought to dominate one another, to be superior, to be the one in control. This was the curse—woman would try to be in control over man, and man would rule over the woman.

This was not the way it was supposed to be. Jesus came to reverse the curse and restore the partnership for the sake of the kingdom!

The liberalist, feminist movement that seeks to dominate men and elevate the rights of women above them happening in some countries isn't reversing the curse—it is still the curse.

The reverse of the curse looks like the kingdom—men and women partnering together, submitting to Jesus, and laying down their lives for the sake of others to put an end the devil's work.

Prayer

> *Father, You created me as a woman to be a strong partner for the work of the kingdom. I am a strong and powerful help to all people, male and female. I am a strong partner for a husband, a leader, a co-worker, a friend, and a child. The power You have given me is not for dominating another or making myself superior to any other person, but for humbly offering my life to advance the kingdom of God. Thank You. In Jesus' name, Amen.*

Activation

Who are the people in your life with whom God has partnered you? Have you been a strong partner? How will you partner in the future? How will you be a part of Jesus' women's movement for the kingdom of God?

DAY 52: GIRL POWER—
THE WOMAN AT THE WELL

Many Samaritans from that town believed in
him because of the woman's testimony,
"He told me all that I ever did."
John 4: 39

Pursue love, and earnestly desire the spiritual
gifts, especially that you may prophesy.
1 Corinthians 14:1

The story of the woman at the well begins in a lonely place at the wrong time of day. Why? The woman at the well didn't want to run into anyone from her church, neighborhood, or family. She didn't want to talk to the Jewish man sitting by the well either. By the end of the story, she is going throughout her town telling her story.

What a difference an encounter with Jesus makes.

Her testimony wasn't actually about the tragedies in her life or a confession of five husbands—her testimony was, "He told me all that I ever did," which means He prophesied to her about her life. He gave her what is called a word of knowledge—detailed information about her life He couldn't have guessed or known. It was divinely revealed. It was a supernatural encounter.

People are hungry for the supernatural. They want to know that God is real. They want to know that God sees, knows, and cares about the things in their lives that they hide from others for fear of being rejected and ridiculed. When Jesus prophesied to the woman about her life, He drew her into worship—a divine encounter with the One who forgives, restores, redeems, and loves.

Pursue love. Look for someone to love, and while you are looking, desire to bring them a supernatural encounter through the gifts of the Spirit, especially prophecy, so that their testimony will shamelessly include, "He [Jesus] told me all that I ever did."

Perhaps your city will be saved.

Prayer

> *Father, You know every person on the earth. You know their stories, their heartaches, their joys. You know their desires and thoughts. You know how You want to love and bless them. Give me the gift of prophecy, words of knowledge, and words of wisdom. Teach me how to serve You and bless others in the use of these gifts. And most of all, Lord, fill my heart with overwhelming love for people. In Jesus' name, Amen.*

Activation

Think about where you will be spending your time today. A coffee shop. A restaurant. A business. Practice listening for words of knowledge by asking the Holy Spirit who you will meet today and what they need. Then bless the people you meet!

DAY 53: GIRL POWER—
THE DAUGHTERS OF ZELOPHEHAD

Then drew near the daughters of Zelophehad…
Mahlah, Noah, Hoglah, Milcah, and Tirzah.
And they stood before Moses and before
Eleazar the priest and before the chiefs and all
the congregation, at the entrance of the tent of
meeting, saying,
"Our father died in the wilderness. He was not
among the company of those who gathered
themselves together against
the Lord in the company of Korah, but died for
his own sin.
And he had no sons. Why should the name of
our father be taken away from his clan because
he had no son?
Give to us a possession among our father's
brothers."
Numbers 27:1-4

It was the end of an era and the birth of a new season. After forty years in the wilderness, a whole generation had died and a new generation was standing on the edge of the Promised Land, ready to enter in. The tribes were gathered for the preparation and reorganization for entry. Of the 601,730 people named, only six were not clan leaders. Five of the six are women. They were the daughters of Zelophehad. The author is intentional here, drawing our attention to something easily passed over, but that something is about to change history.

The greatest danger in front of them was settling for less, settling for a watered-down version of what God had promised, or settling for nothing at all. This was a clear case of gender exclusion. Zelophehad had no sons. He had five daughters. The Promised Land was being distributed to each family. The rule was that if the father of the family had died, the land would go to his sons. If the man had no sons, the land would be given to another family. Daughters did not receive land.

The land represented inheritance of the promises of God. Remember, the Lord said He would give them a land flowing with milk and honey. If the family received no inheritance in the land, their family ceased to have a possession or portion of the promises of peace and prosperity and abundant God-blessed life among the nation. The land was the tangible fulfillment of the promises of God. The company of Korah had sinned against the Lord by rebelling against Moses and the earth opened up and swallowed them, their families, and their possessions. They ceased to exist. They would not receive any inheritance of the promises of God in the land.

Without precedent, in spite of the culture and expectations, and risking rejection from their community, these daughters decide together to speak up asking to be counted among the sons to receive their father's inheritance.

What they were asking for was a change in the law that would require a divine oracle for reformation. It was not really against the rules; it wasn't in the rules. When they stood together to speak up, God stood with them. They paved a way for the generations after them to have what the generations before them did not have! They changed the world for women. Hebrew inheritance laws for women were changed that day and remain to this day. This case in Hebrew history has been named the oldest case still cited as an authority in law courts today.

The daughters of Zelophehad had GIRL POWER! They changed the world as they knew it!

Prayer

> *Father God, these women had such courage to do what had never been done. They changed history. I want this kind of courage. I want to make a difference for the generations of women who will come after me. Position me for influence. Mold and shape my character, my life, my thinking. Teach me Your ways and grow me into the kind of woman others will point to as a model of godly wisdom and courage. In Jesus' name, Amen.*

Activation

What is the promise of God over your life? It is nothing less than the kingdom of God. It is to receive the Holy Spirit and power to bring healing, deliverance, salvation, eternity, and the blessing of God to your family and those to whom you are sent. It is a life lived in God's presence in intimate relationship. It is dreaming God-sized dreams to give birth to God-sized plans! It is to experience the peace that surpasses understanding, the fullness of joy, and the rest that comes from knowing God's complete and constant love for you. It is to receive authority to rule over the enemy and all the works of darkness anywhere, at any time, for anyone.

Is the promise to:

- ☐ Have a healing ministry?
- ☐ Evangelize a neighborhood, a city, a nation, a generation?
- ☐ Teach and preach the gospel?
- ☐ Usher in a new sound from heaven and overtake the music industry?
- ☐ Become a Joseph and finance God projects all over the world?
- ☐ Be sent to comfort the brokenhearted and encourage the faint of heart?
- ☐ Be the next Billy Graham or Joan of Arc or _____?
- ☐ Revolutionize the child protection services or the prison system or the educational system or the medical system?
- ☐ Mentor the next generation of young women leaders, defend abused women, or rescue sex-trafficked women?

How are you dreaming of making a difference and making history? It is time. You *can*. Invite the Holy Spirit to speak to you about where, when, and what you are to speak up for.

DAY 54: GIRL POWER—MARY

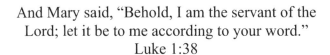

And Mary said, "Behold, I am the servant of the
Lord; let it be to me according to your word."
Luke 1:38

"And blessed is she who believed that there
would be a fulfillment of what was spoken to
her from the Lord."
Luke 1:45

But Mary treasured up all these things,
pondering them in her heart.
Luke 2:19

Mary's story always reminds me that life with God is amazing and full of miracles in the middle of life's difficulties. She was so incredibly brave. When she said "Yes" to God, she said "Yes" to the miraculous. She could not have known that a life of miracles was a life of faith in the face of impossible situations. But then, that is what the miraculous is, isn't it?

Do you believe in miracles?

I was a labor and delivery nurse for many years a lifetime ago. Each time a new life broke through into this old world, I heard the gasp of a new breath taken and the release of a fresh cry for freedom. I knew I'd witnessed a miracle. I have five grandsons. Five is the number for grace. They are each a miracle. A miracle of grace.

My mom is a miracle too. A few years ago, she was diagnosed with cancer. Shocking. Sorrowful. Frightening. There are no words that adequately describe the violation of life that cancer is. It is an ungodly plague. Yet, miracles come in the midst of plagues.

I believe in miracles. The kind that bend the laws of nature and the limits of our mind. The kind that nearly escape notice masquerading as coincidence and the kind that take your breath away for the majesty and mystery of the occurrence. I have experienced each kind and both have deepened my faith and amplified wonder.

I wonder if perhaps the reason some miracles go without being noticed is that the one we hoped for may not be the one we receive. For example, God did not heal my mom the way I wanted. I have seen countless healing miracles in Brazil, Europe, and America. My mom did not receive that kind of miracle. Her cancer was not healed, and she passed away. When this happens, it is a test of our faith. I'm not sure miracles come without a test of faith. Can we recognize the miracle when it comes? After all, some missed the miracle of the Savior who came in a manger.

Will we embrace what comes, trusting that God knows what we cannot, and more than this, that He does only what is right, only what is good? In this, it seems, is not only a test of faith but a revelation of our belief system. What do we believe about the One who does miracles? Is He kind? Is He loving? Is He good? Is He real? Is He here? Does He care? Yes. Yes. Yes. Yes. Yes.

Oh yes, I believe in miracles. I believe in the One who does the miraculous. I don't believe miracles are too incredible, too impossible, limited to medical science, or perhaps left to chance. I believe life itself is a miracle. Every breath, every sunrise, every face.

Let's make a pact. Let's be amazed every day. Let's not ever become so hardened by difficult circumstances that we lose the ability to be amazed.

Prayer

Father, You are the God of miracles and a God of wonder. When we say "Yes" to You and Your miracle-working ways, we are saying "Yes" to trusting You in impossible situations. You do the most marvelous things. You do good things, right things, loving things, kind things. Even when the miracle we were looking for is not what we see, You are still good and working miraculously in our midst. I just want to say thank You today for all the miracles, big and small, hidden and revealed, You have done. More Lord! And I will trust You in each and every circumstance. In Jesus' name, Amen!

Activation

Who needs a miracle today? Invite the Holy Spirit to give you the courage to ask God for their miracle. Go and heal the sick, cast out demons, and raise the dead today, tomorrow, the next day, and every day until it becomes a normal, everyday occurrence! I believe in miracles!

DAY 55: CALL ME MARA

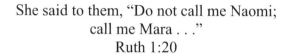

She said to them, "Do not call me Naomi;
call me Mara . . ."
Ruth 1:20

See to it that no one fails to obtain the grace of
God; that no "root of bitterness" springs up and
causes trouble, and by it many become defiled . . .
Hebrews 12:15

Naomi means "pleasant," "abundance," or "delight." In Hebrew culture, a name was an identity. After a season of great loss, Naomi feels lost. She rejects her identity and embraces bitterness. Bitterness is unresolved anger and grief. It opens the door to depression, hopelessness, and despair. It narrows vision. It distorts faith, rejects hope, disowns joy, and distrusts love. Our speech, behavior and relationships become defiled by it. We say and do bitter things we wouldn't normally say and do. We are not ourselves.

Naomi was not herself. In her own words, "I went away full, and came back empty." She was bitter. She had been through a heart-crushing experience. She blamed God. In her bitterness, she told her old friends to call her what she was—bitter. She told her daughters-in-law they would be better off going back to their old lives and their old gods because there was no hope for a future. She told everyone that God's hand was against her.

But it wasn't.

When we read the story, we find something so beautiful, and so full of God's mercy. He preserves her name. He sees past her bitterness, past her anger, and past her grief. He sees Naomi—pleasant, abundant, and His delight. He sees her future and the restoration He would bring her.

Her true identity, the gift and call on her life, was not changed. It was held, with her heart, in the hand of God. She needed healing, not punishment. She needed comfort, not condemnation. She needed restoration, not rejection.

There was a time when my story was a lot like Naomi's, a time when I experienced such difficult and traumatic things that I fell into a bitter depression and was not myself for over a year. I said and did things I would not normally say and do. I was not myself. When I look back on that dark time in my life, I am brought to tears over the kindness of the Lord. There was no lightning bolt, no earthquake, not even a knight in shining armor. But there were moments, conversations, and unusual kindnesses from people around me that awakened my heart to life again.

Ruth did this for Naomi. She was God's gift. God preserved Naomi's gift and call, her name and identity, and sent her a daughter to show her God's lovingkindness. Then, He did the most marvelous thing—He gave her back her name in all its fullness. She walked in her true identity as Naomi, the one who is pleasant and a delight.

Oh, isn't the Lord so good!

Today, are you a Naomi or are you a Ruth?

Prayer

> *Father, Your lovingkindness is without end. In moments of bitterness and grief, You love me, in spite of my wrestlings and ramblings. The Psalmist says that I cannot hide from Your love. I cannot escape Your gaze. Thank You. Where I need healing, comfort, and restoration today, Lord, I invite You into those places. Restore my vision and my identity. In Jesus' name, Amen.*

Activation

- Are you a Naomi today?

  - Invite the Holy Spirit to show you those the Lord has given you to be like Ruth in your life. They are loyal and steadfast friends who do not reject you when you have rejected yourself, who do not stop believing in the call on your life when your vision is narrowed, who do not walk away from you when you refuse to be hopeful, joyful, or trusting.

  - How does it make you feel to know God has been preserving your true identity while you are entertaining bitterness and unresolved anger?

- Are you a Ruth today?

  - Invite the Holy Spirit to show you who in your life is in a Naomi experience.

  - How can you show them the lovingkindness of God?

DAY 56: BITTER INTO SWEET

And he cried to the Lord, and the Lord showed
him a log and he threw it into the water and the
water became sweet.
Exodus 15:25

It had been only three days since the Israelites had crossed the Red Sea, pursued by Pharaoh and his fearsome army. God had miraculously parted the sea. They had all escaped, the oldest to the youngest, even those with four legs. Pharaoh's army tried to follow, but were swallowed up in the sea. On the other side of breakthrough, Miriam had led the celebration, with shouts of, "The horse and the rider have been thrown into the sea." It was the greatest deliverance the world had ever seen.

Three days later, the Israelites find themselves in the wilderness, thirsty and needing a drink. They come to the waters of Marah. Stagnant and poisonous, they could not drink them.

It's not at all what the people were expecting. It's not at all what the readers of the story are expecting. It sort of knocks the wind out of us, pulls the rug out from under us, stops us in our tracks. It stopped them in their tracks too.

They grumble. They get stuck in their mind and blocked in their hearts so that they can't move on. "They soon forgot his works; they did not wait for his counsel," says the Psalmist (Psalm 106:13). Even though they had experienced the miracle of the Red Sea, even though the Lord was with them as a pillar of cloud by day and a pillar of fire by night, they grumble. Their default response to adversity is negativity.

Research shows that negativity and complaining rewire our brain until we don't even realize we are doing them. It becomes our habit. Over time, it is easier to be negative than positive, regardless of what is happening around us. Complaining becomes our normal behavior, which then changes how people around you perceive you.

We are called to be God's holy people, a royal priesthood. We are supposed to be sign and a witness and a blessing to the surrounding nations, the revelation of God to a corrupt and perverted world (1 Peter 2:9-10).

The bitter waters were a test for the people of Israel, a test meant to grab their attention so God could reveal something new about Himself to them. It was something they would need to know about who He is and what He would be for them as they move forward.

He is the God who turns the bitter into sweet. Today, He wants to get you unstuck. He wants to remove negativity that has become a habit, because it is your time to shine!

Prayer and Activation

> *Father, in the name of Jesus, I come to You to confess and receive deliverance, healing, and a renewed mind. You say that when we come confessing that the way is opened to refreshing, that when we ask You to forgive, we are forgiven, and that Your mercy is new every morning. You said that we are not to be conformed to this world, swayed by culture and its sensitivities, philosophies, and mindsets. But, Father, we are those who take every thought captive unto Jesus Christ, who has overcome the world and taken back the keys of authority over all things in heaven, on earth, and under the earth. And I am His child, friend, and co-heir. I am in Him and He is in me. Jesus was neither negative nor ignorant of the enemy's devices, and neither am I to be.*
>
> *Therefore, in the name of Jesus and by the power of the Holy Spirit, I come out of agreement and alignment with:*
>
> ☐ *a spirit of fear and anxiety*
> ☐ *unresolved anger*
> ☐ *a spirit of disappointment*
> ☐ *a victim mentality*
> ☐ *a religious spirit*
> ☐ *a political spirit*
> ☐ *fatalistic thinking*

- □ *a spirit of unforgiveness*
- □ *a spirit of bitterness*
- □ *doubt and unbelief of every kind*

I ask You to forgive me for agreeing with the lie from the pit of hell that told me nothing will ever change. Forgive me for speaking negative words over my body, spouse, relationships, city, state, nation, church, and church leaders. Now, I take authority over and break the spirit of negativity off my mind and release a rewiring of my brain so that when I receive breakthrough, set out in the new thing, and face adversity or hardship, I will not default to negativity, grumbling, and complaining, but I will look and see to hear the new way the Lord is going to work on my behalf, the new word He has for me, the new revelation and understanding He wants me to have that will turn the bitter into sweet. Now Holy Spirit, come. Fill me up right now. Fill up every empty place. Fill me afresh with confidence and peace, love for God, myself, others, and my enemies. Fill me with hope and contentment. Make me fearless and determined once again. In Jesus' name, Amen.

DAY 57: COME TO THE TABLE

The Lord is my shepherd; I shall not want.
He makes me lie down in green pastures.
He leads me beside still waters. He restores my
soul. He leads me in paths of righteousness for
his name's sake. Even though I walk through
the valley of the shadow of death,
I will fear no evil, for you are with me;
your rod and your staff, they comfort me.
You prepare a table before me in the presence of
my enemies; you anoint my head with oil; my
cup overflows. Surely goodness and mercy shall
follow me all the days of my life,
and I shall dwell in the house
of the Lord forever.
Psalm 23

"My sheep hear my voice."
John 10:27

How different would our lives be if we heard the voice of God personally and intimately for our lives? Hearing the voice of God in the darkest time in my life changed me forever. It saved my life and my marriage. It brought me into a relationship with God I didn't know I could have.

We have learned that God speaks through the written Word of Scripture. Psalm 23 is one of the most personal and beautiful of all the Psalms. In these verses, we hear the reassurance of God that we are not alone in our journey. He is with us every step of the way. He guides us, leads us into times of rest and restoration, and relieves our fears and anxieties in difficult and dangerous seasons. In those times when the enemy attacks and accuses, He brings us to His table to partake and participate in worship, healing, and victory.

There is *more*.

God also speaks a spoken word of revelation that can come to our ears or our hearts. He will come as the Great Shepherd, bring us to His table in the presence of our enemies, and say, "Look at me. Look at my face. Do not look at your situation. Do not listen to the voice of a stranger. See me and hear my words over this situation."

He desires to deepen your intimacy with Him in order to increase your ability to hear His voice, personally and directly, and to encourage, build up, and comfort you and all those around you.

Prayer

> *Father God, You are the God who speaks. You have created me to hear Your voice. Bring me to Your table and increase my ability to hear Your voice personally and directly. In Jesus' name, Amen.*

Activation

Read Psalm 23 slowly and invite the Holy Spirit to bring it alive for you personally. Picture yourself sitting at a large table with the Lord. Invite the Holy Spirit to speak to you over a situation in your life where you need reassurance or guidance.

Write down the things you see and hear. How did you feel while you were sitting at the table with the Lord? How did the Lord apply the Scriptures to your situation? What guidance did you gain from Him?

DAY 58: DEVELOPING A LISTENING EAR—AWARENESS AND PURSUIT

"He who has ears, let him hear."
Matthew 13:9

"But blessed are your eyes, for they see,
and your ears, for they hear."
Matthew 13:16

We want to be women who hear His voice personally and directly. Over the next few days, we are going to intentionally develop a listening ear.

In Mathew 13, Jesus says the people do not hear because their hearing had grown dull. They were not expecting nor seeking to hear God's voice. They were not looking for God in their present, day-to-day lives. When Jesus showed up, they were not aware that God was in their midst and speaking to them.

To have ears that hear means that we have a heart that is awake to God and open to receive, perceive, and understand what God is saying. In other words, developing a listening ear begins with awareness and pursuit. We start with the awareness that God is a speaking God. *He is speaking today!* Hebrews 1 tells us He spoke in the past and is still speaking. Hebrews 12 warns us not to reject His voice. God has given us the gift of the Spirit and the ability to hear His voice.

When we become aware that God is speaking, we can be intentional about pursuing His voice. God awakens our ears to hear, but we have the responsibility to grow in our ability to hear by developing a listening ear:

> The Lord God has given me the tongue of those who are taught,
> that I may know how to sustain with a word him who is weary.
> Morning by morning he awakens; he awakens my ear to hear as
> those who are taught. The Lord God has opened my ear, and I
> was not rebellious; I turned not backward. (Isaiah 50:4-5)

Isaiah tells us to intentionally listen for the voice of the Lord God, because those who hear become wise and are able to speak into the lives of others so they can keep moving forward with God and in the purposes of God.

Prayer

Father God, You created me to hear Your voice. You are always speaking. I am not always listening, but I want that to change. Open my heart and my ears to hear You afresh. Give me an awareness of Your presence and Your voice. Right now, I am choosing to pursue You. I am pursuing hearing Your voice. Help me develop a listening ear! In Jesus' name, Amen.

Activation

Take a few moments to ask the Lord if you have any unbelief regarding His ongoing desire to speak to His people, and repent of any doctrine or belief that denies God speaks today.

Create a strategy for reminding yourself throughout the day to look and listen for His voice.

Pay attention to thoughts and physical, spiritual, and emotional stirrings, and ask the Holy Spirit if He is speaking.

DAY 59: DEVELOPING A LISTENING EAR— INTIMACY AND TIME

"No longer do I call you servants, for the
servant does not know what the master is doing;
but I have called you friends, for all that I have
heard from my Father I have made known to you."
John 15:15

See what kind of love the Father has given to us,
that we should be called children of God; and so we are . . .
1 John 3:1

In the beginning, God created the heavens and the earth so He could create us. He created us in relationship with Himself and for relationship with Himself. He is the Father who lives in covenant community within Himself, as Three-in-One in unbroken fellowship. He created us to be family, friends, sons, and daughters.

Hearing God's voice comes out of intimacy with God. Intimacy with God means we have a relationship with Him in which we experience His presence and hear His voice. We develop a two-way, conversational relationship, a friendship anchored in love and trust. In the context of this relationship, we become familiar with His voice.

To cultivate intimacy, we have to spend *time* with Him in His presence. When we spend consistent and intentional time with God, we become familiar with His presence, His voice, His ways, His Word, and the way He communicates to each of us individually. Over time, we grow our ability to hear the voice of God in the midst of silence, chaos, crisis, celebration, distraction, suffering, danger, and deadlines.

Scripture reading and meditation, worship, daily devotions, and prayer help us cultivate an intimate relationship with God and increase in us a sensitivity to His presence and His voice (see Psalm 130:5-6, Isaiah 50:4-5, Habakkuk 2:1).

Prayer

Father, You created me because You love me and want to be close to me. You are pursuing me for a relationship, a friendship, a family. You want to talk as friends, as family, as a Father to the daughter whom You love. I want that too. Deepen our intimacy this year until what Jesus said is true of my life— that I am His friend. Take me deeper in love with You. Show me Your ways, surround me with Your presence, and speak to my heart. In Jesus' name, Amen.

Activation

Have you ever considered that the Lord would want to have the kind of friendship with you in which He could share His secrets with you? How would that make you feel? What kind of time can you set aside to become friends with God? How will you use this time?

Invite the Holy Spirit to speak to you about deepening your intimacy with God and how He desires for you to partner with Him in it. Write it down and begin the journey into God's presence!

DAY 60: DEVELOPING A LISTENING EAR—
LOVE AND THE HEART OF GOD

…the Lord appeared to him from far away.
I have loved you with an everlasting love;
therefore I have continued my faithfulness to you.
Jeremiah 31:3

"As the Father has loved me, so have I loved
you. Abide in my love."
John 15:9

God is love. Everything He says and does comes out of His love. Even correction and discipline come from a heart full of love. Most of us have experienced these things coming from a heart full of anger, disappointment, or rejection. This creates fear, and fear is a block to hearing.

When God delivered the people of Israel from their bondage to Pharaoh, He brought them to Mount Sinai to speak to them. But when God came near, they became afraid and "stood far off" (Exodus 20:18). They refused to get closer and listen. They told Moses to listen for them (see Exodus 20:18-20). This was never God's heart.

Then came our precious Jesus. He saved us from sin and Satan and sickness. He healed the wound in our relationship with the Father, and showed us His great, immeasurable love toward us. We are now children of God, loved beyond measure. The writer of Hebrews now proclaims we have not come to the terrible mountain where the thunder and fire of God terrified even Moses, but we have come instead to a joyous gathering of angels and to the city of heavenly peace where we are citizens by the blood of Jesus (see Hebrews 12:22-24). We are invited in to the holiest of holy places, into the very presence of God to find mercy and grace for every need. Nothing can ever take us out of the loving security of God's hand (see Hebrews 4:16, 10:19; John 10:29).

Have you ever been on a plane? Before takeoff, the flight attendants instruct us how to care for ourselves in case of an emergency. The oxygen mask will drop down, and we are to place it over our nose and mouth and breathe. Then we are told a surprising but important bit of information. If we have children with us, we are to put our own oxygen mask on first before helping the child. Why is this? If we do not put our own oxygen mask on first, we may lose consciousness before we are able to help the children, and both of us will suffer the consequences.

Knowing God's heart and hearing His voice are like having oxygen. They allow us to breathe and truly live. In order to express the Father's heart and voice to others, we must first know His heart and voice for ourselves. It is vitally important. Hearing God's voice comes easily when we know and trust His heart.

Prayer

> *Father, show me Your heart. I want Your perfect love that casts out all my fear. Let me taste and see that You are good. Let me experience Your loving kindness in tangible ways. I look forward to hearing Your voice and knowing Your heart. In Jesus' name, Amen.*

Activation

Ask the Lord to tell you how He loves you. Invite the Holy Spirit to show you God's heart for you.

DAY 61: DEVELOPING A LISTENING EAR—ASK AND LISTEN

Therefore Eli said to Samuel, "Go, lie down,
and if he calls you, you shall say, 'Speak, Lord,
for your servant hears."
1 Samuel 3:9

And David inquired of the Lord, "Shall I go up
against the Philistines? Will you give them into
my hand?" And the Lord said to David, "Go up . . ."
2 Samuel 5:19

Call to me and I will answer you, and will tell
you great and hidden things that you have not
known.
Jeremiah 33:3

"Ask, and it will be given to you; seek, and you
will find; knock, and it will be opened to you.
For everyone who asks receives, and the one who
seeks finds, and to the one who knocks
it will be opened."
Matthew 7:7-8

These are some of my most favorite Scriptures. They assure me that God not only speaks, but is waiting eagerly for me to ask Him to speak—about anything and everything!

In the Old Testament, kings, priests, and prophets would inquire of the Lord for answers and direction in the time of war, famine, or expansion. They were the ones anointed with the Holy Spirit. The Holy Spirit would come upon than and enable them to hear revelation.

Now we are the anointed ones who can hear the voice of God. The Holy Spirit not only comes upon us, but lives in us. He inhabits us. He knows everything and can tell us "great and hidden things" we do not know. "Great and hidden things" is another way of saying God will give us revelation, the things we can't find out on our own, either by research or intelligence. Scripture says His thoughts are higher than ours. We just cannot think, see, and understand the way He does. However, He is ready and available to speak to us on any subject to share what only He knows, sees, and understands.

And here is the key: ask and then listen.

We find all throughout Scripture that men and women of God not only made requests—they also made inquiries. Most of us have been taught to pray. We talk to God. We ask Him to work on our behalf. We make requests. Many of us however, have not learned to develop a listening ear by asking a question and waiting for an answer.

Prayer
> *Father, You are all-knowing and all-seeing. Your thoughts are higher than mine. You search the minds and hearts of men. You know the way of the world. You know the past, present, and future. There is nothing You cannot reveal to me. You have the answers I need. Speak, Lord, Your servant is listening! In Jesus' name, Amen.*

Activation

What is the biggest question on your heart today? Write it down with today's date. Invite the Holy Spirit to speak to you about your question. Now wait on the Lord for His answer.

If the answer doesn't come today, do not be discouraged. This is why you wrote down the question and a date. Spend some time listening for the answer to your question each day until you hear. God always answers in His own timing.

Answers to questions can come in many ways, because God speaks in many ways. Be looking for His answer from His still, small voice, a vision or dream, or a conversation with another person. Invite the Holy Spirit to make you aware of the answer when it comes.

———————⟨◇⟩———————

DAY 62: DEVELOPING A LISTENING EAR— OBEDIENCE

"Everyone then who hears these words of mine
and does them will be like a wise man who built
his house on the rock."
Matthew 7:24

But be doers of the word, and not hearers only,
deceiving yourselves.
James 1:22

"As for that in the good soil, they are those
who, hearing the word, hold it fast in an honest
and good heart, and bear fruit with patience . . .
Take care then how you hear, for to the one who
has, more will be given, and from the one who
has not, even what he thinks that he has will be
taken away."
Luke 8:15,18

Obedience to what we have heard opens us up to further revelation. Why? Hearing equals listening and obeying. Revelation is progressive. God will give us a little to see what we do with it. Each time we act on what we have been given, He gives more.

What does this mean for us? It means that an immediate personal obedience brings an increase in revelation and hearing. It is just that simple.

Think about it. Have you ever worked alongside someone who said they loved the job and wanted to be a leader, but they never fulfilled the tasks they were given? What happened? They were not trusted with more.

Hearing God's voice is a stewardship. When He shares His heart, direction, and intentions with us, are we responding in obedience? If not, He is not punishing us, but He is surely waiting for us to respond and obey in order to give us more.

And remember, partial obedience is actually disobedience. You can find this truth by reading the story of Saul in the Old Testament.

We develop a listening ear by developing an immediate obedience to His word.

Prayer

Father, You want to show me many things. You desire to give me more revelation and speak on more subjects. My obedience is an act of worship. You ask me to obey not because You are controlling, but because it is a gateway to revelatory experiences and greater exploits. I choose to obey. Speak Lord, and I will obey Your word. In Jesus' name, Amen.

Activation

We never want to give the enemy a chance to take us captive to introspection so that we are spending our time condemning ourselves or allowing our thoughts to be host to the accuser. However, we do want to be open to the loving conviction of the Holy Spirit and allow the kindness of the Lord lead us to repentance. True repentance is a change in the way we think, which then changes the way we live our lives.

Invite the Holy Spirit to show you anywhere where you have not walked in full obedience. Ask Him what the root of the problem is.

- ☐ If it is sin, ask God to forgive you. He is ready and willing!
- ☐ If the root of the problem is wounding, ask God to heal you. He is ready and willing!
- ☐ If the root of the problem is a lie you have believed, ask God to replace it with truth. He is ready and willing!
- ☐ If the root of the problem is fear, ask God to come with his perfect love and cast it out.
- ☐ If the root of the problem is demonic bondage, come out of agreement with it, take authority over it, break its power, and tell it to *go*.

171

Whatever the root problem is, God is ready and willing to uproot it! Let the Holy Spirit show you the root, how God desires to remove it, and then invite Holy Spirit to fill you up in that place.

When this is completed, invite the Lord to speak to you about next steps. Then practice immediate obedience!

DAY 63: DEVELOPING A LISTENING EAR— KEEPING A CLEAN HEART

Therefore, as the Holy Spirit says,
"Today, if you hear his voice,
do not harden your hearts as in the
rebellion, on the day of testing
in the wilderness, where your
fathers put me to the test and
saw my works for forty years.
Therefore I was provoked with
that generation, and said, 'They
always go astray in their heart . . .'"
Hebrews 3:7-10

"And blessed is the one who is
not offended by me."
Matthew 11:6

And he said, "Are you also still without
understanding? Do you not see that whatever
goes into the mouth passes into the stomach and
is expelled? But what comes out of the mouth
proceeds from the heart, and this defiles a
person. For out of the heart come evil thoughts,
murder, adultery, sexual immorality, theft, false
witness, slander. These are what defile a person
. . ."
Matthew 15:16-20a

My daughter, Nicole, was a beautiful baby. I loved her so much, but it seemed like nothing I said or did would soothe her. My other children always responded to my voice. I would speak in whispers, laugh with gusto, and even sing silly songs and worship over them. They would laugh and listen to my voice. But Nicki was different. She could not settle.

One day, just a few weeks after she was born, I noticed a gooey, green liquid in her crib near where her head had been laying. When I examined my sweet baby closer, I realized it was coming from her ears. It frightened me. I took her to the doctor and he discovered that due to the trauma of her delivery, she had developed a serious infection in her ears. For months, we battled that infection. When it was finally healed and cleared, she responded to my voice in the same way her brother and sister had.

Just like Nicki, when we have an infection in our hearts, we cannot respond to God's voice. It infects our ears, blocks our hearing, and distorts our attitude, disposition, and behavior. Bitterness, unforgiveness, offense, anger, etc. filter and skew what we hear, how we interpret what we hear, and how we speak what we hear.

In Matthew 11, Jesus warns about taking offense toward Him. John the Baptist has been arrested and put in prison. He has done nothing wrong. Jesus doesn't seem to be doing anything to help and John, and His followers have the opportunity to be offended over it. The word used for "offense" can be interpreted as "tempted to unbelief." If they give in to the temptation, then they will not be able to hear Jesus's words and understand His message.

Keeping a clean heart keeps our ears clear and open. It allows us to hear and to speak the words of the Lord without distortion.

Prayer

> *Father, today I come and ask You to search my heart. I pray with David in Psalm 51:10, "Create in me a clean heart, O God, and renew a right spirit within me." I want to have a clean heart, and ears that are clear so that Your word to me and through me will be clean and undistorted. Thank You. In Jesus' name, Amen.*

Activation

While we do not want to be distracted with compulsive self-evaluation, we do want to be open to the Spirit's convicting work. Invite the Holy Spirit to search your heart and guide you in dealing with anything that will hinder your ability to hear Him and operate in healthy prophetic ministry.

DAY 64: DEVELOP A LISTENING EAR— COMPETING VOICES

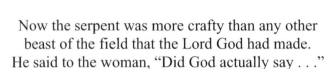

> Now the serpent was more crafty than any other
> beast of the field that the Lord God had made.
> He said to the woman, "Did God actually say . . ."
> Genesis 3:1

> Beloved, do not believe every spirit,
> but test the spirits to see whether they are from God,
> for many false prophets have gone out into the world.
> 1 John 4:1

God's voice is not the only voice we have the ability to hear. There are other voices competing for our attention. The voice of the serpent (the enemy), the voices of those around us, and the voice of our own flesh all want to be heard. Developing a listening ear means we learn to recognize and discern His voice from all the others.

Eve's story is the first, but not the last, story of a person listening to a competing voice. When she listened long enough, she became convinced and turned from the voice of God. This is what got her into trouble. In Scripture, voice equals authority. Authority is the power to rule and make the decisions. When Eve listened to the voice of the serpent and turned from the voice of God, the enemy gained authority or control in her life. God is the only one who deserves to have a say in who we are, what we think, and what we do. He is trustworthy and can be entrusted with authority over our lives.

Discerning His voice from the voice of the enemy begins with recognizing that God is the same yesterday, today, and forever (see Hebrews 13:8). He does not lie, twist, or distort truth. There are some things God will not say. He is not accusing and condemning, though He will correct and warn. He is always good, always loving, always just, and always forgiving, merciful, and gracious. Recognizing His voice means becoming aware of His nature and character, which will always be evident in His words.

Identifying and discerning God's voice apart from our own is a bit more difficult. This requires time and experience. Often when our heart's desires are involved, it can be difficult to separate God's voice from our own, whether we are listening for ourselves or someone else. Further, there are times when our love and compassion, anger and resentment, logic and reasoning, or even our imagination, are louder than the voice of God. As a result, we may give our own word, not God's.

It is important to always check our hearts on every matter where our emotions are involved. Maturity and accountability are how we overcome our lack of discernment. Becoming intimate with the Scriptures is another safeguard.

Finally, all prophecy is to be judged. Judged simply means that prophecy is to be evaluated or tested to discern if it is God speaking. The Bible says not to quench the Spirit or look down on prophecies, but to test everything. If something is good, hold it fast. If something looks evil, keep away from it (see 1 Thessalonians 5:19-20).

Prayer

Father, I want to become so familiar with Your voice that I can hear it in the midst of ten thousand other voices. I want to hear what You have to say on every matter. Even when my heart is attached by an affection to a person or situation, Lord, I want to hear Your voice so that they receive the revelation of heaven for their lives. I want the same for my life too! In Jesus' name, Amen.

Activation

Have you received a prophetic word from someone or from your listening time? Let's practice evaluating the voice it came from. To properly evaluate prophecy, we ask and answer a few questions[6]:

☐ Does it agree with the whole counsel of the Word of God?

A prophetic word needs to line up with Scripture. Contemporary prophecy is not equal to Scripture, and the Holy Spirit will not disagree with Himself.

☐ Does it agree with the nature and character of God?

☐ Does it produce an inner witness in the one receiving the word?

We are to discern of what spirit a prophetic word is. Discernment is the ability to judge a situation or a person, and the ability to distinguish between different types of spirits (angelic, human, demonic) and motivations (evil, good).

☐ Do the leaders have an inner witness regarding the word and agree with it?

Now that you have applied these simple tests, is this a word of the Lord to you?

❮◇❯

---

[6]Evaluation of prophecy through testing is not for the purpose of shaming, condemning, humiliating, or criticizing. People who are genuinely attempting to be Spirit-led and walk in the supernatural gifts need to feel safe, loved, and encouraged even as prophecy is evaluated. In this way, evaluation becomes a healthy part of the prophetic operations of a prophetic community.

DAY 65: DEVELOPING A LISTENING EAR— GOD'S WORD

So faith comes from hearing,
and hearing through the word of Christ.
Romans 10:17

Let the word of Christ dwell in you richly,
teaching and admonishing one another in all
wisdom, singing psalms and hymns and spiritual
songs, with thankfulness in your hearts to God.
Colossians 3:16

All Scripture is breathed out by God and
profitable for teaching, for reproof, for
correction, and for training in righteousness, that
the man of God may be complete, equipped for
every good work.
2 Timothy 3:16

It had only been a short time since I had had a radical encounter with the Holy Spirit that turned my world upside down. I had heard His voice for only the second time in my life. I knew I had received a call to ministry. I knew what He wanted me to do for the next five years. He had given me very specific instructions. He had said, "Get out a notebook. Get a pen. Open your Bible to Hebrews chapter 10 verses 19-25 and 35-39. These are your life Scriptures. Every day for the next five years, you are to read your Bible, pray, study your Bible, and journal." He was that specific. It was to be my training, the preparation for what was coming.

I did everything He asked. I began to notice a dramatic change. The more I read and studied Scripture, the clearer the voice of the Lord became. When I was with other people, a verse would come to my mind. I would simply tell the person, "I keep hearing this verse. Does it mean anything to you?" They would laugh, cry, or be amazed. It was an answer from God.

As my hearing and gift of prophecy developed, I realized something else—that the measure or test of what I was hearing and prophesying is God's written Word. It is prophecy. It is the voice of God in writing. It is the measure of everything else we will hear as we develop our listening ear.

Reading the Bible and allowing its truth to saturate our minds and hearts gives us insight and understanding into who God is—His ways, words, and heart. It increases our ability to hear His voice about our lives and circumstances. It is essential for developing a listening ear.

In my own life, reading the Bible was key to developing my ability to hear God's voice confidently. True prophetic revelation is always in agreement with God's written Word and is the primary way we test prophecy.

Prayer

Father God, Your voice is Your Word. Your written Word is revelation. It is prophecy. It is truth. It is the measure of all other revelation and truth. It is the foundation for hearing Your voice and prophesying Your Word. Create in me an insatiable hunger for Your Word. Holy Spirit, illuminate the Word of God to me so that it may dwell in me and bring a rich harvest. In Jesus' name, Amen.

Activation

Invite the Holy Spirit to show you the face of someone you know who needs encouragement today. Now invite Him to lead you to a passage of Scripture for them. Once you have the verse or verses, invite the Holy Spirit to show you what this passage means, and what it will mean to this person. Write it all down. Find a card and write down the passage of Scripture and what the Lord, by His Spirit, showed you about it. Give the card to the person and watch what happens!

DAY 66: DEVELOPING A LISTENING EAR— LOVE FOR OTHERS

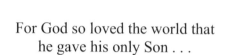

For God so loved the world that
he gave his only Son . . .
John 3:16

We love because he first loved us. If anyone
says, "I love God," and hates his brother, he is a
liar; for he who does not love his brother whom
he has seen cannot love God whom he has not
seen. And this commandment we have from
him: whoever loves God must also love his
brother.
1 John 4: 19-21

It is easy to develop a listening ear when we have a heart full of God's love. The Lord is eager to speak to people. He gave us the Holy Spirit and the gifts so we would be exceptional in the encouragement, edification, and comfort of others. He has equipped us to introduce others to a God who is real, present, working, and desires reconciliation and ongoing relationship.

Love is primary. It is to be the motivation for all that we do. When our hearts are full of God's love, our heart will be full of love for others.

Once, I was sitting in my church. There was a man sitting a few rows behind me. He was not dressed well. His hair was a mess. His clothes were sloppy. He was tattooed and pierced and very thin. He looked very uncomfortable. My heart was becoming passionate for him to know Jesus, the God who loves him so much He died for him. As I allowed the Lord to stir up my compassion, I began to listen for God's voice. It came to my heart that this man had disqualified himself from receiving God's pardon and love because of the things he had done. He did not feel he deserved love. He was sure that if he opened his heart and made his story known, he would be condemned, judged, and punished. But this was not God's heart for him. As service ended, I stood to go to him, but a close friend of mine was already speaking to him.

Later that afternoon, she called me and told me the story. She had felt the same things from the heart of God. She had been moved with compassion and love for him. She had heard he had disqualified himself because of his past. And so she told him about God's heart and words and he welcomed her prayers.

Prophecy always expresses and reveals the heart of God—His loving nature, His loving agenda, and His loving will. Opening our hearts to the love of God for others develops our listening ear.

Prayer

> *Father, Your heart is so full of love for all people. You loved me before I could love You. You love them in the same way. Jesus, You gave Your life for us all, even when we were still in sin and did not believe in You. Break my heart for others. Give me a passionate love for people that will open my ears to hear Your words of love, compassion, reconciliation, and redemption for them. Put Your words in my mouth and let me prophesy. In Jesus' name, Amen.*

Activation

Invite the Holy Spirit to bring to your mind someone you know or have met recently who is not close to the Lord or doesn't know the Lord at all. Ask Him to speak to you about where they are and what might be the block to their coming into relationship with Jesus. Ask Him to give you a prophetic word about the love of God for them. Write it all down.

Reflect on what you heard. Did it change the way you feel or see the person? Did it stir up compassion in your heart? Did it create a desire in you to be able to listen for others you will meet?

DAY 67: DEVELOPING A LISTENING EAR— IMPRESSIONS

Pursue love, and earnestly desire the spiritual
gifts, especially that you may prophesy.
1 Corinthians 14:1

In the beginning, God created the heavens and the earth with a word. He spoke and created the earth with all its color and variety. He spoke and created mankind. No two persons are alike. Every people group has its own language and way of communicating. In what language does God speak? How does He communicate? He speaks with color and variety! He speaks in ways that cross all language barriers. We were created to hear His voice.

To develop a listening ear, it is important that we have an understanding of what we are listening for! We are listening for God's voice, and sometimes this does not involve hearing with our created ears, but rather hearing by the Spirit.

God speaks in many ways. Therefore, there are many ways in which we receive revelation from God. Over the next three days, we will learn several common ways God speaks. You may find that you have been receiving revelation for a long time but did not know how to recognize it!

Today, we focus on the most common way we recieve revelation: impressions (2 Kings 2:15; Luke 8:45-46; Acts 14:9, 27:10). An impression can be mental, emotional, or physical.

Mental impressions often come like sudden, fleeting, seemingly stray thoughts—a name, Scripture, or idea that comes to mind.

Have you ever left the house, had a sudden thought to go back inside and get a certain object, but ignored it—only to realize later that you needed that very thing? Very often this is the Holy Spirit giving you an impression.

Emotional impressions typically feel like a sudden experience of an emotion not connected to your own situation.

When I was fairly new to prophecy, I received an emotional impression while visiting a women's ministry meeting. There were about a hundred or more women in the room, and I was seated somewhere in the middle. The speaker on the platform was talking about how doing fifteen minutes of housekeeping each morning, especially in the kitchen, was proven to increase the desire to maintain household organization. However, I found that I was having a hard time listening to the speaker. I felt grief, anxiety, and a deep ache in my heart, though I had nothing in my life to warrant it. I began to ask the Lord where these emotions were coming from. Suddenly, I understood that several women in the room were suffering over marital problems and prodigal children. They were aching to receive encouragement and ministry for these things. Though I was unable to do anything with this impression, both because I was a visitor at the church and because I lacked training in prophetic ministry, it was an experience I was able to refer to later on as I grew in recognizing emotional impressions.

Impressions can come through the five senses—sight, touch, taste, smell, and hearing.

A common example of a physical impression is when you suddenly feel pain or a physical sensation of some kind that you know does not belong to you. This is often a type of word of knowledge—specific information divinely revealed.

I received such a physical impression once while sitting on a platform and observing the Lord move in a group of women as they worshipped. Suddenly, my feet felt like they were on fire! I tried to stand, but the fiery pain only increased. I started to panic, and then realized I was receiving an impression—a word of knowledge—for someone in the room. As a former nurse, I understood that the pain I was experiencing was neuralgia. "Is there anyone in the room suffering from neuralgia in your feet?" I shouted. "It is a pain that feels like your feet are on fire, and it hurts to stand. The Lord wants to heal you!" Four women stood up. Two were immediately healed, and two received a major touch of the Lord in their bodies as we prayed for them.

Impressions can come as pictures either to the natural eye or your mind's eye.

On one occasion, I stepped up to the platform and turned around to begin preaching. Suddenly, for a brief moment, I distinctly saw a musical note above the head of a young woman. It disappeared, and a Scripture came to mind: Zephaniah 3:17. When I told her what I saw, she immediately laughed and then cried. It was her life Scripture. God was reminding her that He sings and rejoices over her.

Impressions can come by touch, as when you come into physical contact with a person. The impressions come to the mind, but are activated by touch. In my own life, there have been many times when I do not have a sense of what God is saying to someone until I put my hand on their shoulder.

Impressions sometimes come as a taste or smell—something that is not actually manifesting in the natural, but is a spiritual, divine revelation. Many people have reported smelling roses when angels are in the room or rotting flesh when demons are present. Similarly, when an actual sound in the natural comes to your ear, such as a voice, a song, or a train passing by, the sound can activate a prophetic impression and understanding in your mind.

Remember, impressions are usually subtle and can be easily dismissed. Awareness is the first step to developing our listening ear for impressions.

Prayer

> *Father, You are the God who speaks. I am Your child and I want to develop a listening ear. Today, Lord, give me a new sensitivity to the Holy Spirit and prophetic impressions. Awaken in me an awareness of subtle impressions coming through my senses, and into my thoughts by Your Spirit as I go about my day. As I begin to trust these impressions are from You, bring me quick confirmation to build my confidence. In Jesus' name, Amen.*

Activation

Take some time to reflect on the past few days. In circumstances and in conversations, can you identify any impressions in thought or emotion that were later confirmed in some way? Had you considered these were from the Holy Spirit?

Think about the day ahead: the people, places, and events you will meet. Ask God right now to give you an impression about any of them. Check your body, emotions, senses, and thoughts. Write down what you receive. Then, go throughout your day watching for confirmation. Remind yourself throughout the day to be aware of impressions regarding people or circumstances that may quickly cross your mind or senses.

When you receive confirmation, ask the Lord to show you if there is any action to take to impact the person, place, or event on His behalf.

DAY 68: DEVELOPING A LISTENING EAR— DREAMS, VISIONS, & ANGELIC VISITATIONS

Let the prophet who has a dream tell the dream
but let him who has my word speak my word
faithfully.
Jeremiah 23:28

The Bible is filled with spectacular stories of divine encounters through dreams and visions, and angelic visitation. Moses, Joshua, Gideon, and Daniel were visited by angels. Jacob, Daniel, Joseph were dreamers. These encounters gave direction, affirmation of identity, coming events, and more. Those who received them were strengthened and encouraged, and often moved to bold action. Sometimes, their hearts were broken for the things that break God's heart, and always, they became closer friends of God as God shared His secrets with them.

Along with dreams, visions, and angelic visitation, listed below are a few other creative ways in which God speaks to us. For many, dreams, visions, and the ways listed below are the primary way of receiving revelation from God. Perhaps they are yours as well!

Dreams (Genesis 20:3; 1 Kings 3:5-15; Matthew 1:20, 2:13, 2:20). Dreams are visions in the night that come during sleep. Not all dreams are from the Lord. They can come from our own soul because of something we are dealing with in our emotions, or they can come from the enemy as a form of warfare or attack. They can be literal, which means they interpret themselves. They can be filled with symbolism and need careful and Spirit-led interpretation. Dreams can bring warning, direction, insight, wisdom, or a prophetic message.[7]

---

[7]There are many good books and programs to become equipped in dream interpretation. If dreams are a primary way you receive prophetic revelation, it is important to know the correct way to interpret them!

Several years ago, I had a dream. In the dream, I was dressed in a pink tutu and a black leotard. I was my actual age, so it felt pretty silly. I was standing just offstage at a college with two other people dressed in leotards. There was an audience and a woman with a clipboard. In the dream, I knew that I was being considered for specialized training for a specialized dance. The woman with the clipboard asked the three of us to do our best ballet moves across the platform and back. We each did. I did terribly, but I was relaxed and having so much fun. Suddenly the woman I did not know turned around and looked at me, and I knew I had been chosen. Then I woke up.

Upon waking, I received the interpretation from the Holy Spirit. The Lord was choosing me and sending me back to school for specialized study, which would bring me into a new life with the Holy Spirit. An hour later, I received an invitation to apply for a doctoral program to study the supernatural gifts of the Holy Spirit with Dr. Randy Clark. The rest is history.

Visions (Genesis 15:1; 2 Kings 6:17; Ezekiel 1:1; Acts 2:17, 11:5; 2 Corinthians 12:1). Visions can be very short or very long. They can be mental pictures—simple, fleeting images in your mind's eye. Or they can be scenes that unfold like a movie on the screen of your mind with a divine message.

Open visions are visions that are seen and received with the open, naked, natural eye.

Once during a time of prayer, I saw a vision of a brightly hued, enormous dragonfly, which flew to my feet. I climbed on its back and it flew to a field filled with flowers. I "knew" we were to gather pollen. Moving from flower to flower, I gathered with my arms until I was covered in bright, mustard-colored pollen. I was laughing and joyful, and the Lord said, "It's time for cross-pollination." The vision ended. Within weeks, I was introduced to key leaders in other "streams" of the Pentecostal, charismatic, and renewal movement and invited to participate in various events and studies. I was initially invited because of my Foursquare affiliation, and further invited because I had embraced God's word to me. Cross-pollination had begun.

Angelic Visitation (Acts 9:3-7; 27:23-24). An angelic visitation is simply a way of saying an angel revealed itself to you and spoke or showed you a message of some sort.

Creation (Genesis 1:14; Psalm 19:1-6; Acts 2:1-21, Romans 1:20). God often reveals signs of the times and His glory, nature, and faithfulness through what we witness in creation. God can speak through natural circumstances such as meteorological and astronomical events, geopolitical events, and economic events.

Puns/Parables (Jeremiah 1:11-12). Puns and parables are symbols or sayings the Lord releases that require prayer and interpretation. A pun is a play on words in which a word or a picture can mean more than what is obvious. Puns are like messages wrapped in a puzzle or joke. Parables are messages wrapped in short stories.

A friend of mine came to ask my help in interpreting a vision she recently had. In the vision, she had gone into her boss's office. When she was there, a very large elephant walked in. It was dressed up like those on parade in India.

It was a pun. The Lord was showing her that there was an elephant in the room between her and her boss that needed to be addressed. In American idiom, "an elephant in the room" means an issue that everyone is aware of but nobody is addressing or talking about.

Trances (Acts 11:5, 22:17; Revelation 1:10-20). Trances are an experience in which you are awake, yet your awareness of your natural surroundings is suspended (or transcended) and all your senses and focus are drawn toward observing a vision or event. Your body is present in the natural, but your mind and spirit are caught up "in the Spirit" in an intense revelatory experience.

Prayer

Father, speak to me in visions and dreams! Give me the gift of interpretation of dreams just as You did for Daniel (Daniel 1). I acknowledge today all the creative ways in which You speak and are still speaking. Open my eyes and ears in the daytime and at night to receive revelation. Visit me in my dreams and send angels with Your words and wisdom! In Jesus' name, Amen.

Activation

Put a pad of paper and a pen near your bed. Before falling to sleep, invite the Holy Spirit to use your dreams to speak into your life and the lives of others. Upon waking, immediately record any dream you had the night before. Ask the Holy Spirit what it means. Seek the Bible and other respected godly resources for interpretation of your dreams. (Do not inquire regarding interpretation from occultic or witchcraft sources).

Here are a few suggestions for help:

☐ Gen. Ed Leland Ryken, James C. Wilhoit, Tremper Longman III, *Dictionary of Biblical Imagery*, (Downers Grove, IL, Intervarsity, 1998).

☐ Resources on dream interpretation by John Paul Jackson, Mark Virkler, Barbie Breathitt, Doug Addison, James Goll, and Dr. Paula Price.

DAY 69: DEVELOPING A LISTENING EAR— THE WORD AND THE VOICE OF GOD

My sheep hear my voice.
John 10:27

And we have the prophetic word more fully confirmed,
to which you will do well to pay attention as to a lamp shining in a dark place,
until the day dawns and the morning star rises in your hearts, knowing this
first of all, that no prophecy of Scripture comes from someone's own
interpretation. For no prophecy was ever produced by the will of man,
but men spoke from God as they were carried along by the Holy Spirit.
2 Peter 1:19-21

When people ask me my personal secret to hearing God's voice, I tell them I read Scripture. Our Bible is the record of the words and thoughts and heart of God. I have found *nothing* that activates my ability to hear God's voice better than reading Scripture. Why? Because it makes me familiar with the sound of His voice, the way He speaks, and the things that are precious to His heart.

God spoke and men recorded His words. His recorded words are powerful and still active. God loves to speak to us through His written Word. Just as He spoke to men and women found in Scripture, He speaks to us today by His own voice to our heart and mind.

Here are two very important ways God speaks.

Scripture (Luke 24:45; Romans 16:4, 25-26; 2 Timothy 3:16, 2 Peter 1:19-21). Receiving a Scripture is a common way of receiving revelation. While praying, reading, or speaking, a particular passage will suddenly be highlighted to you. It seems to "jump off" the page or become emblazoned on your mind's eye, and you feel stirred in your spirit over it. There is suddenly a fresh understanding in your mind and heart regarding what the Lord is communicating in that particular moment to a particular person or circumstance.

The Voice of God (1 Kings 19:13; Luke 3:22; John 10:27; Acts 9:3-7). God speaks in our language as well, whether it is English, French, Chinese, Portuguese, or Hindi. He spoke to His kings, prophets, Son, and apostles. Jesus says, "My sheep hear my voice" (John 10:27).

The voice of God can be experienced as a still, small voice heard by the heart, or as an audible voice heard by the ear. The former is the most common experience with the voice of God, but many have heard the audible voice of God. I am one of them. I was sitting in my living room reading my Bible, while my children slept in the next room. Suddenly, and very unexpectedly, I heard the audible voice of God. Though I knew what He said, the sound was all around me, inside and out, and it was more like a rumbling than a human voice. It was awe-inspiring, and it demanded, without any words, a response in the form of a decision to obey or not.[8]

Prayer

> *Father, there is no limit to Your creativity. Your voice is heard in so many wonderfully creative ways. My spiritual ears and eyes are designed to hear Your voice. I want to experience all the ways You speak! I want to be Your friend and share Your heart. I want to hear Your secrets. Speak, Lord! I am listening! In Jesus' name, Amen.*

Activation

Invite the Holy Spirit to bring to your mind a friend He knows needs encouragement. Write down the name of the person. Ask the Holy Spirit to speak to you through Scripture about and for this person. What passage of Scripture describes how God sees them? What passage of Scripture do they need to hear and hold onto today? Ask the Holy Spirit why He chose those particular passages and what they will mean to the person. Consider writing the passages in a card and explaining what the Lord wants them to understand

---

[8]I tell this story in its entirety on Day 1: My Story in this Activational.

through the passages of Scripture. Then send it to the person the Holy Spirit put on your heart.

Reflect on each of the ways God speaks discussed over the last three days. Recall stories from your own life in which you heard God's voice in any of these ways. Which of the ways God speaks listed above have you not experienced but would you like to? Why? Ask God to speak to you in new ways and take note when He does!

DAY 70: DEVELOPING A LISTENING EAR— PROPHETIC JOURNALING

Thus says the Lord, the God of Israel:
"Write in a book all the words that I have spoken to you."
Jeremiah 30:2

Jeremiah, Isaiah, and many other prophets wrote in a book all the words God spoke to them. They were, of course, writing Scripture. We are not writing new scripture. The words we hear do not have authority equal to Scripture. However, the words of the Lord are still worth keeping track of for our lives for the purpose of developing our listening ear.

Developing a listening ear requires practice. Practice may not make us hear perfectly, since we can only see through a glass darkly this side of heaven, but it certainly will cause us to grow like crazy. We can all think of things in our lives that we've needed to practice to become good at them. Becoming aware of the ways God speaks and learning to listen well is a process for all of us.

Prophetic journaling is a practice I have used for many years to develop my ability to hear God's voice and receive His words for myself, friends, family, strangers, cities, and even nations. Even after twenty-plus years, I still practice prophetic journaling.

There is another reason I journal. From the moment I first heard God's voice, I have wanted to keep a record of the things God says to me and the ways He fulfills His word. I want my children and grandchildren one day to be able to read through the record of God's faithfulness, miracles, and kindness to me and, in turn, to them. I was changed by His voice. When I am gone from this life, I want my family who never knew me to be changed as well. I want them to read the record of the supernatural ways God works and be hungry to hear His voice just as I was.

Prophetic journaling involves two important practices: First, listening and journaling what you hear at least three times each week (daily is best), and second, doing a personal evaluation at the end of each week.

Before you begin, make it an adventure. Begin by choosing the right journal for you! Consider size, weight, line spacing (if lined at all), binding, and even style. Remember, size and weight matter if you plan to travel with your journal—even if only to the coffee shop! Line spacing, binding and even color can be distracting and discomforting. Let the color and style of the journal "speak" to you about the season you are in. Be creative!

Prayer

Father, Your words have value to me. To hear Your voice has great worth. I want to hear Your words and increase in my ability to hear. Awaken my ear to hear and I will write them in a book. Help me to create a written record of Your faithfulness, Your goodness, and Your miraculous workings in my life. Let it record Your voice and the words You fulfill in my life. In Jesus' name, Amen.

Activation

For Daily Practice:

- ☐ Invite Holy Spirit to speak to you about your day.
  - o What to expect—the day's happenings
  - o How to co-operate with what He wants to do
  - o What are you to focus on today?
- ☐ Ask Him what you are to prophesy over your day. Say whatever He says! Record the "word" in your journal.
- ☐ Record all prophetic experiences.
  - o What prophetic words and Scriptures you do you "hear" for yourself or others?
  - o What dreams did you have in the night?
  - o What visions or pictures did you receive?
- ☐ Record your level of awareness of God's presence.
- ☐ Record any questions you have in regards to the prophetic and ask God to speak to you about them. Record what He says.

For Weekly Evaluation:

- ☐ Review this week's daily entries.
- ☐ Were there any words, or parts of words, fulfilled?
- ☐ What is the Lord doing in you?
- ☐ What are you learning?
- ☐ What are the challenges you are encountering?
- ☐ How have you seen God moving in your life and the lives of people around you?
- ☐ What is the overall message God has given you for this week?
- ☐ Is there any further action that should be taken in response?

DAY 71: THE GIFT OF PROPHECY

And in the last days it shall be, God declares,
that I will pour out my Spirit on all flesh,
and your sons and your daughters shall
prophesy,
and your young men shall see visions,
and your old men shall dream dreams;
even on my male servants and female servants
in those days I will pour out my Spirit,
and they shall prophesy.
Acts 2:17-18

The prophet Joel prophesied that God would pour out His Spirit, and that men and women, both young and old, would prophesy, dream dreams, and see visions (Joel 2:28-29). He saw that in the future, God would answer Moses' prophetic declaration: "Would that all the LORD's people were prophets, that the LORD would put his Spirit on them!" (Numbers 11:29). Isaiah also prophesied the Holy Spirit would be put upon God's people, and His words of power and revelation (prophecy) would be in their mouth for all generations to come, to eternity (see Isaiah 59:19-21).

When we receive the baptism, or infilling, of the Holy Spirit for empowerment, we receive the gift of prophecy. He is the source and resource of all the spiritual gifts. They are His power and ability manifesting in and through us (see 1 Corinthians 12, Romans 12). The gift of prophecy is for everyone! Peter said so, and Paul also tells us, "For you can all prophesy one by one, so that all may learn and all be encouraged" (1 Corinthians 14:31).

Prophecy is hearing God's voice and saying what He is saying. I love what Abraham J. Heschel says about prophecy: "The invisible becomes audible."[9] In other words, God tells us about things we cannot see or know, and we get to tell others!

---

[9]Abraham J. Heschel, *The Prophets*, 2 Vol. in 1 (Peabody, MA: Prince Press, 2004), ix.

Prophecy is a gift. The gift of prophecy, like the gift of the Holy Spirit and salvation, is a free gift (Romans 5). You cannot earn it, but you can eagerly desire it! Paul tells us, "Pursue love, and earnestly desire the spiritual gifts, especially that you may prophesy" (1 Corinthians14:1).

Prayer

> *Father, in the name of Jesus, I thank You I have the Holy Spirit living in me. Thank You for the gifts of the Spirit that are part of Your life in me through the Holy Spirit. Stir up this gift and open my heart to receive revelation! I am deciding today to pursue the gift of prophecy. In Jesus' name, Amen.*

Activation

Invite the Holy Spirit to bring to mind someone you love. Ask Him to speak to you about how much He loves them. Pray they come to know the love of God in the ways the Spirit revealed it to you. Consider writing and sending these thoughts in a card of encouragement to this person.

DAY 72: PROPHECY AND GOD'S HEART

"For God so loved the world that he gave his
only son, so that whoever believes in him, should
not perish, but have eternal life. For God did not
send his Son into the world to condemn the
world, but in order that the world might be
saved through him."
John 3:16-17

I was just leaving the platform after preaching when a young woman came to me with a friend she wanted to introduce to me. It was the friend's second time visiting the church, and she wanted to thank me for the message. I immediately felt the Holy Spirit and knew the Lord wanted to speak to this girl about her life. I looked her in the eye and asked, "Where are you at with the Lord?"

She stuttered and stumbled, clearly unsure of how to respond.

"Would you say you know the Lord as your Savior?"

"No!" she said immediately.

"Would you say you are a Christian?"

"No," she responded passionately. "I am not religious or spiritual at all!"

"I want you to know that Jesus is running after you," I responded. "He has watched over you for all of your life. He wants you to know you are loved. You have not felt loved growing up, but you are. He wants you to know what it feels like to be loved, and He wants to show you that your life not only has value—He has a purpose for your life."

She started to cry.

"Do you want to ask Him into your heart to be your Savior so you can receive His love?" I asked.

"Yes!" she said.

Right then and there, I led her to the Lord in prayer.

Jesus told us that the Holy Spirit would tell us what He hears from God and about things in the future (see John 16:12-14). God told Jeremiah, and all of us, to ask Him, and He would tell us about important things we could never know or find out on our own (see Jeremiah 33:3). Paul says if an unbeliever hears prophecy, his heart will be convicted and convinced as the secrets of his heart are revealed. As a result, he will fall down on his face, worship God, and say, "God is truly among you" (1 Corinthians 14:24-25). Through prophecy, God's heart is revealed to those who do not yet know Him.

The real God has a real heart. When we think about the heart of God, what do we think about? Sometimes people think a lot of things about God that are not true—mostly because someone did not represent God's heart well in their words or actions. God longs to reconcile, save, heal, deliver, rescue, and restore people. He wants them to know that He created them for better things than sin and death, and He has good works for them to do. He wants them to know He has a plan for their lives, and that He sees past their past, forgives sin, and erases doubts and regrets.

Prayer

> *Father, I want everyone to know You, especially my family and friends. I can see that the gift of prophecy shows them You are real and that You have a heart of love for them. I want to show people Your heart. I want to know Your heart and I want to know Your heart for the people in my life. Give me revelation knowledge and speak to me about Your heart for others. Use me and the gift of prophecy to bring others into relationship with you. In Jesus' name, Amen.*

Activation

Make a list of the people you know who do not yet have a relationship with Jesus. Invite the Holy Spirit to give you God's heart for them. Ask Him to speak to you about what they need to know and hear from God in order to see that God is real. Write it all down. Ask the Holy Spirit to give you an opportunity to tell each of them what you have heard. Ask Him to soften and prepare their hearts to be drawn to the Lord.

DAY 73: PROPHECY'S PURPOSE

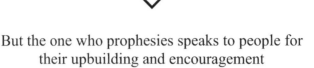

But the one who prophesies speaks to people for
their upbuilding and encouragement
and consolation.
1 Corinthians 14:3 ESV

But the one who prophesies speaks to people for
their strengthening, encouraging and comfort.
1 Corinthians 14:3 NIV

Prophecy's primary purpose is to strengthen or build up, encourage, and comfort others and the church. God will use us to speak words that give courage, hope, and confidence to a person or people, which will help them to move forward, receive increase from Him, or grow. This means God will use us to speak words that give a person boldness, purpose, and the courage to overcome fear and intimidation. It means God will use us to speak words that comfort people in times of suffering or relieve their worry and fear.

I was walking out the door of Atlanta International Airport to the parking lot when I noticed a woman sitting in a wheelchair. I had *that* feeling. After all these years and countless experiences, I recognize the nudges of the Spirit and have become vulnerable to His leading. I began a conversation under my breath, "Oh man, are You going to ask me to pray for her healing?"

No response.

"Lord, if You want me to pray for her, have her turn around and notice me just like I noticed her."

At that very moment, the woman's phone rang and went flying out of her hand. I leaped to help this poor impaired woman—until she jumped out of the wheelchair to grab her phone and answer the call. A minute later, she hung up and turned her attention to me. Laughing, she said, "A lady left this when she got picked up—I just decided to borrow it while I wait."

Suddenly, in my mind (or maybe it is my heart—I do not know for sure, but I know I perceive it on the inside, like a whisper or a fleeting thought), the Lord said, "I want you to tell her she is a leader to her family. Her voice is influential and what she has to say to them is important. It will be heard."

I told her exactly that, except that I prefaced it with, "You may think this is sort of strange, but sometimes I feel like the Lord speaks to me for people. I feel like the Lord wants you to know—"

Her eyes got wide. "I just flew in to Georgia from another state because my family is in crisis. I came to have a meeting with them and speak into the situation."

I asked if I could pray with her.

"Yes!" she cried. As I prayed, tears filled her eyes. Afterward, she kept thanking and hugging me.

The word from the Lord gave her courage and confidence. It was a word that "encouraged, built up, and comforted" just as God intended, according to Paul in 1 Corinthians.

Prayer

> *Father, I want to be used to strengthen others, instill courage in them, and offer them the comfort only You can give. You have given me the gift of prophecy and You have said I hear Your voice. Speak to me today about the circumstances and situations going on in the lives of people I meet today. Strengthen them, encourage them, and comfort them—through me! In Jesus' name, Amen.*

Activation

Invite the Holy Spirit to give you an awareness you can feel when He wants to speak to you and through you to others. Throughout your day today, keep the question, "How do you want to strengthen, encourage, or comfort this person?" in your mind. When a strengthening, encouraging, or comforting thought comes to your mind, tell them what you are thinking. Simply say, "I feel like maybe the Lord wants you to know _____." Watch people get strengthened, encouraged, and comforted!

DAY 74: WORDS HAVE POWER

Life and death are in the power of the tongue.
Proverbs 18:21

Did you know that your words can release actual power—the power of life or death? All those within hearing of your speech, including yourself, are affected. Even the environment is affected! In other words, if you speak death, things die. *But* if you speak life, things live!

In the New Testament, Jesus said, "But I tell you that every careless word that people speak they shall give an accounting for it in the day of judgment" (Matthew 12:36-37). *Ouch*! Why would Jesus say this? Let's look a bit closer. In the Greek, a careless word is a word that does no good "work." It doesn't accomplish the powerful things God gave us words to accomplish! Our words have real power to change things. We can send them out to "work" a good work and bring life to circumstances, relationships, bodies, and even geographical places!

It has been said somewhere that women speak 25,000 words a day. What if we used each and every word to work a miraculous change in every person, place, and circumstance around us? 25,000 words. 25,000 life-bringing, miracle-working, power-releasing words.

I had a friend who was newly pregnant. She had been pregnant before, but suffered the loss of that baby. She started bleeding and the doctor told her she was losing this baby too. He told her to go home and wait for it to happen. When she called to tell me, my spirit rose up in me and joined with the Holy Spirit. I knew that Scripture says life and death is in the power of my tongue. So I didn't need to beg God or timidly ask. *No!* I could stand in confidence that it is God's will to give life, and just speak life. So that is what I did. I began to stomp around my house and speak life over her pregnancy, her body, and her baby. The bleeding stopped, and her baby boy was born perfectly healthy months later. Glory to God!

Today, make a commitment to be careful, not careless, with the words you speak. Be a woman whose words release power to bring life into every dead and dying situation you encounter!

Prayer

> *Father, in the name of Jesus, thank You for giving me a powerful tongue! My words are powerful and bring life! Today I commit to use my powerful words to speak life over every place, person, and circumstance I come into contact with. Holy Spirit, come! Give me new opportunities to use my words to bring life each and every day, wherever I am and to whomever I am with. In Jesus' name, Amen.*

Activation

Take some time to ask Holy Spirit to bring to your mind places, circumstances, and people that are dying in some way, need to come to life, or come back to life.

With the understanding that your words have power to release life, simply speak "LIFE" over each one in the name of Jesus.

Example: In the name of Jesus, I speak LIFE over _____! LIFE! LIFE! LIFE!

DAY 75: CREATIVE PROPHECY

> …as it is written, "I have made you the father of
> many nations"—in the presence of the God in
> whom he believed, who gives life to the dead
> and *calls into existence the things that do not exist.*
> Romans 4:17 [emphasis mine]

The earth was created by the word of the Lord. In the beginning, there was no earth (Genesis 1:1-2). God didn't need anything to work with. He is the Creator God. He speaks a creative word, and something comes out of nothing. Oh, our magnificent, all-powerful God! God's word releases creative power. Isaiah the prophet tells us God's word never returns empty and unfulfilled, but always accomplishes the purpose for which He sends it (Isaiah 55:10-11). God's speech, the word that comes from God, releases creative power.

Prophecy, the words God is speaking about the present and the future, contains power to create and carry all things forward on their appointed course to the fulfillment of God's will and plan. When we speak what He is speaking about the present and the future, we are used by God to release His power to transform people and circumstances.

We are calling things that are not as though they are (Romans 4:17). Again, God's word never returns unfulfilled. Prophetic words call the future into being, and call the present into kingdom perspective and under kingdom rule for transformation to take place according to God's will.

In other words, prophecy releases the power of God's word to create divine atmospheres, attitudes, thinking, visions, and plans, etc. that are not yet in existence. What does not yet exist can be called into existence by the power of the prophetic word. Time to *prophesy*!

Prayer

Father, You are the creator God. You speak and what does not exist comes into existence. You speak and something is created out of nothing. Nothing is too hard for You to do and nothing is to wonderful for You to do. You are in me by Your Spirit. Your words are put in my mouth by the Holy Spirit. The Spirit of my Father, the Lord of all creation, speaks through me. I align my heart with Yours. I give You my eyes and my mouth right now. Give me Your perspective to see what does not yet exist in my life, the lives of others, and the places where You have planted, and sent me that You desire to exist and I will prophesy it by faith, in Jesus' name. Amen.

Activation

Invite the Holy Spirit to speak to you about yourself, others, situations, circumstances, and places. What does not yet exist in your sphere of influence that God desires to bring about? Make a list and then declare them as though they exist!

Example: "I prophesy right now to the nation of Brazil that you have a righteous government with leaders who fear and please God and care for the people. I prophesy that it is blessed in finances, blessed in leadership, and blessed in health."

DAY 76: THE SPIRIT OF PROPHECY

"For the testimony of Jesus is the spirit of prophecy."
Revelations 19:10b

What is your powerful testimony?

What has Jesus done for you? What have you seen Him do in your life, the lives of your family members, your work or business, or your body, mind, heart, and perspective? Anytime you have been a witness to something Jesus has done, it is yours to give away in testimony.

Testimony is the spirit of prophecy. Prophecy is the word of the Lord spoken or written. Prophecy releases the power of God over people, places, and situations to create and accomplish the thing it speaks of. God does not value or love one person more than another, even if one has more beauty, education, wealth, or social status. What He does for one person, or in one situation, or in one place, He is able and willing to do it in another similar situation, for another person or place.

So, whatever you have witnessed personally and have to give as a testimony, it can be used as prophecy to call into existence what is not yet in existence, to bring creative power for transformation, and to release a new divinely ordered future over people, places, and situations.

Prayer

> *Jesus! You have done so many things in and around me—big things, little things, healing things, relational things, financial things, heart things, things for me, things for those around me, things I asked for and things I did know to ask for, things I needed, things I wanted, and things You simply wanted to do to bless me. Thank You, thank You, thank You! Now Lord, I know what You have done for me and for others, You will do again for many more. I ask that, as I testify to all I have witnessed,*

You release Your prophetic power to those who will hear it, and to every situation and place over which I declare it! In Jesus' name, Amen.

Activation

With a journal in hand, invite the Holy Spirit to bring to your mind everything you have witnessed Jesus do, first in your own life, and then in the lives and places around you.

Each "thing" listed is a testimony and the content of a prophetic word. Read them over slowly and give God thanks for each and every one.

- For each testimony listed, ask the Holy Spirit to bring to your mind a person, place, or situation that needs to hear it and receive the prophetic power it carries.
- Ask the Holy Spirit to create an opportunity to give the testimony to each person.
- Go give the testimony and pray with the person declaring that God will do for them what He did for you!

Watch God move! When He does, you have another testimony!

DAY 77: NAMING REALITY

The natural person does not accept the things of the Spirit of God,
for they are folly to him, and he is not able to understand them
because they are spiritually discerned
1 Corinthians 2:14

The prophetic names reality from heaven's perspective. In order to recognize the opportunities for kingdom advancement in the coming days, we must see the changes, even and especially the geo-political ones, from God's point of view.

In Genesis 1:26, God creates mankind in His own image. Being made in God's own image comes with "response–ability," the ability to respond. It is the essence of faith. Faith is a response to revelation. In Genesis 2:19-20, we find Adam's first assignment and words. Context reveals not only God's perspective on the circumstances, but also His plan of action. Adam was alone, it "was not good," and God would bring the solution. Yet, rather than act alone, God invites Adam to participate, giving him the opportunity to perceive what God already perceives.

God brings animals to Adam to "see" what he would name them. The word used for "see" in this passage is the Hebrew word *ra'ah*, which has a prophetic component. It is seeing to perceive with a divine perspective. In other words, Adam's first recorded assignment was to *identify* and *interpret* what God had done. Accordingly, he gave God's creative work (animals) names, and in the process, he gained divine perspective regarding the reality of his own circumstance. This prepared him to receive God's plan and solution.

In essence, Adam prophesied the names of the animals according to what he perceived. He was forth-telling—identifying and interpreting the revelation of what God had done in the present. He named reality. Reality is *not* what we see with the natural eye, it is what God has done and is doing manifested in present circumstances. Naming reality is identifying and interpreting

211

the revelation of what God has done and is doing in order to prepare for what He will do. This is forth-telling. This is a powerful function of prophecy.

As people filled with the Holy Spirit, we have the power to *name reality* for others: to identify and interpret what God has done and is doing, thus giving divine perspective to natural circumstances, times, and seasons making room for God's preferred future.

Prayer

> *Father, there are people and circumstances all around me who need heaven's perspective, Your perspective. They need to know what You are doing, where You are working, and Your dreams for the future. I accept my responsibility to name reality from Your perspective. Give me the prophetic gift of forthtelling. Increase my ability to see and know what You are saying and doing. Give me boldness to reframe and name reality according to Your heart, mind and will. In Jesus' name, Amen.*

Activate

Ask the Holy Spirit to open your eyes to *ra'ah*. What do you see politically, socio-economically, and culturally for the church, for the family, for the individual from God's perspective? Write it down. This is your prayer assignment from the Lord!

DAY 78: RESPONDING TO PROPHECY

Man shall not live by bread alone,
but by every word that comes from the mouth of God.
Matthew 4:4

"Have you received a prophetic word for your life? What have you done with it?" This is the question I recently asked my students in an online prophecy course. Not surprisingly, a large number of them responded with something like, "I've done nothing, really. I am waiting for it to come to pass."

Receiving a prophetic word requires an active response. It is serious business!

We are to be people who do not "live by bread alone but by every word that proceeds from the mouth of God." We have all been created in the *Imago Dei* (Image of God). This means we choose whether or not we will come into alignment and agreement with what God says and does. In other words, we have been given the "ability to respond," and therefore a "responsibility," on our end.

There certainly are prophetic words that are unconditional, meaning they will come to pass completely as a sovereign act of God. Most of these are contained in the prophetic promises of God in Scripture. However, nearly all the personal prophetic words we will receive are conditional in nature, meaning we have a responsibility to meet in order that they are released in fullness into our lives.

Our responsibility is to respond to a prophetic word by testing the word, agreeing with the word, praying it through, and acting on it. This type of lived-out strategy releases the power and potential of the prophetic words you receive! Watch and see what God does as you begin the journey!

Prayer

Father, forgive me if I have been negligent in anyway with the prophetic words you have spoken to me personally, or through others. I commit to take them seriously and respond to them responsibly. In Jesus' name, Amen.

Activation

Recall a word of prophecy given to you.

1. Write out the prophecy word for word.
2. Test word by asking questions. Does the word line up with Scripture? Does it resonate in your spirit? Does it rightly represent the revealed nature and character of God? Do those who have been placed in your life for accountability and leadership agree with it?
3. Pray over the word. Make it personal as you pray. Declare it over your life as if it has already come to pass!
4. Create a plan of action, and then, act!

DAY 79: SILENCING THE VOICE OF THE ENEMY

Now the salvation and the power and the
kingdom of our God and the authority
of His Christ have come, for the
accuser of our brothers has been thrown
down, who accuses them day and night before
our God.
Revelation 12:10

"He [the devil] was a murderer from the
beginning and does not stand in the truth
because there is no truth in him . . .
he is a liar and the father of lies."
John 8:44

"My sheep hear my voice."
John 10:27

How many of us are oppressed with thoughts that come to our mind that accuse, condemn, or torment? How many of the people we love are held captive to the lies of the devil?

We can distinguish the difference between the voice of God and the voice of the enemy by simply knowing the character and nature of God, and His Word in Scripture. When the thoughts of our mind and the voice we hear in our heart brings condemnation, accusation, fear, and torment, it is *not* God.

We have the right to silence the enemy. We have the power to stop his lies and accusations. He has been cast down by Jesus. When Jesus died for us, every debt was paid and the right of the enemy to continue to accuse and condemn us was taken from him. All of his lies are swallowed in the love of God in Christ Jesus, exposed and canceled by the shed blood of our Savior.

Not only that, Jesus told His disciples that His sheep hear His voice. We are His sheep. Acts 2 tells us the Holy Spirit has been poured out on all flesh, and from now on all God's people will dream prophetic dreams and prophesy. The simplest definition of prophecy is to hear God's voice and say what He is saying. In other words, we all have the enablement of the Holy Spirit to hear God's voice and prophesy.

When we listen to the voice of God and prophesy what He says over ourselves and others, it breaks the power of the enemy's lies.

Prayer

> *Father, every word that comes from Your mouth is good and right and life. I want to hear Your voice and prophesy. Thank You that You have given me the weapon of prayer and prophecy to combat every lie of the devil in my life and in the lives of those I love. You say the accuser has been cast down and I have the right to silence him. Therefore, in the name of Jesus, I silence the voice of the enemy. I break the power of his lies and his accusations by the true Word of God, the shed blood of Jesus, and the power of the Holy Spirit. You will not speak to me in Jesus' name. Amen!*

Activation

Invite the Holy Spirit to fill you afresh and open your ears, eyes, and heart to hear the voice of God. Ask the Lord to bring to your mind all those who are living under the false accusations, condemnations, and torment of the enemy—perhaps even a people group in your nation.

Write out a declaration prayer, similar to the one above, adding their names and any passages of Scripture the Lord brings to your mind. Then, *declare it over them!* Watch their lives begin to change!

DAY 80: COMING IN THE OPPOSITE SPIRIT

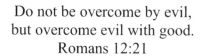

Do not be overcome by evil,
but overcome evil with good.
Romans 12:21

"As for you, you meant evil against me,
but God meant it for good, to bring it
about that many people should be kept alive,
as they are today."
Genesis 50:20

What if I told you that anything the enemy brings against us, we can turn around by prophesying, praying, and moving in the opposite spirit? I hope you would get excited! It is true.

For a long time, many thought the best way to do warfare against the enemy was to deal with demons and the devil himself. Unfortunately, many of them became so focused on the enemy that they lost their ability to see what God was doing.

God and the devil are not equal. God is the Creator; the devil was created. Jesus has gained back all authority on earth, under the earth, and in heaven. Nothing is left outside of His control or power. He is bigger, better, and the only One worthy of our focus, faith, and worship.

Coming in the opposite spirit means that we identify places in our own lives or the lives of others where sin or another work of the enemy is having its way. We know this is not from God or His Holy Spirit. Often, the enemy will work in a way opposite to what the Lord has anointed and called a person, people, or a circumstance to accomplish. Coming in the opposite spirit means we pray, prophesy, and act according to the Holy Spirit in whatever way is the direct opposite to what the enemy is doing. In this way, we are bringing an exchange, a reversal, a turnaround of the things the enemy meant for evil and releasing God's good instead.

Prayer and Activation

Make a list of the negative, destructive, unhealthy, or ungodly emotions, habits, and thoughts in your life—things like fear, depression, addiction of any kind, pride, greed, lust, etc.

- ☐ Invite the Holy Spirit to show you the "opposite." What characteristics, nature, and fruit of the Spirit are the opposite of each of the things on your list?
- ☐ Create a list of the opposites and pray them as declarations over your life.
- ☐ Decide on an action that reinforces the opposite and do it.

Example: "In Jesus' name, I have a garment of praise, not the spirit of heaviness. Praise is rising in my life and all heaviness is broken." Then spend a few minutes praising God.

Now make a list of the negative, destructive, unhealthy or ungodly emotions, habits, thoughts the Holy Spirit reveals to you that plague the lives of the people in your life. (*Remember*, God is trusting you to use this list *only* to pray and prophesy over them in the opposite spirit in private. It is *not* for you to point out to these people their errors and sin, or to do the work of the enemy for him by condemning and accusing them).

- ☐ Invite the Holy Spirit to show you the "opposite." What characteristics, nature, and fruit of the Spirit are the opposite of each of the things on your list?
- ☐ Create a list of the opposites and pray them as declarations over their lives.
- ☐ From now on, treat them as if the opposite is true already. In this way, you overcome evil with good in their lives.

Now, expand your vision to your family lines/households, neighborhoods, cities, and nations. Make a list of negative, destructive, unhealthy, or ungodly practices, activities, laws, mindsets, or beliefs that are prevalent in those places.

- ☐ Invite the Holy Spirit to show you the "opposite." What characteristics, nature, and fruit of the Spirit are the opposite of each of the things on your list?

☐ Create a list of the opposites and pray them as declarations over those places.

———————⟨◇⟩———————

DAY 81: SECRETS OF THE HEART

But if all prophesy, and an unbeliever or
outsider enters, he is convicted by all, he is
called to account by all, the secrets of his heart
are disclosed, and so, falling on his face, he will
worship God and declare that God is really
among you.
1 Corinthians 14:24-25

Years ago, the Reverend Billy Graham, one of history's greatest evangelists, came to the town where I live. I went to see him. His message was clear and easy to understand. Hundreds of people walked to the altar that day to receive Jesus as their Lord and Savior. It was amazing.

I admired him so much, but I knew I was not Billy Graham. I have never felt much like an evangelist. When I was younger, it made me nervous. It felt awkward. I always felt guilty about that. I didn't know why. Other people simply walked up to strangers, started a conversation, and within minutes they would be praying a prayer of salvation.

Then I began to hear the voice of God.

I have a close friend named Nick who also hears God's voice. We were getting something to eat at a nearby restaurant, and when we walked through the bar to our table, he stopped. He walked over to a man and a woman sitting at the bar with drinks. He said to the woman, "You might think this is strange, but I feel like God is saying you are in a bad relationship right now and the three relationships you had before this wounded your heart. Jesus wants to heal you and give you a new relationship." The man next to her, who turned out to be her brother, jumped up and said, "That's true!" The woman did not give her life to Jesus that day, but her brother did.

Through prophecy, God becomes real to those who do not yet know Him. It is a beautiful tool of the Lord for evangelism. We all hear God's voice. We can all do the work of an evangelist.

When God speaks through prophecy to people about who they are, what He sees happening in their lives, how He feels about them, and what He has planned for them, they want to know Him!

Prayer

> *Father, You know the secrets of people's hearts. You have a good plan for their lives and it includes salvation. As I go about my day, every day, share with me the secrets of their hearts so that they will know You are real, You love them, and You are ready to save them. Break my heart for the lost until I cannot wait to share Your love and words with them. Give me a greater ability to hear Your voice and prophesy so that people will desire to know and worship You. In Jesus' name, Amen.*

Activation

Invite the Holy Spirit to bring to your mind someone you know who does not yet know the Lord as their Savior. Ask Him to reveal the secrets of their heart that will make Jesus real to them. Ask Him to show you how He loves them and the kind of future He has for them when they give their lives into His hand. Write down what He s⌁
heard.

Consider writing what you hear in a card, or making a visit to them.

DAY 82: RAISING SUPERNATURAL CHILDREN

> Train up a child in the way he should go;
> even when he is old he will not depart from it.
> Proverbs 22:6

> You have built a stronghold by the songs of
> babies. Strength rises up with the choruses of
> singing children. This kind of praise has the
> power to shut Satan's mouth.
> Psalm 8:2 Passion Translation

My daughter was standing in the hallway staring into her sister's room. She seemed mesmerized.

"Molly, what's going on?" I asked.

"There is an angel standing by Nicki's bed."

Many children who see into the spirit, prophesy, or dream dreams at an early age are misunderstood and discouraged from developing their gift. Many of them never recover the use of the gift no matter how old they get, even if they are part of a church. But God has ordained praise, prophetic proclamation, and worship of His majesty from the mouths of children to silence the enemy and put His adversaries to shame.

God speaks to children. He gives them dreams and opens their eyes to see into the spirit realm. He fills their mouths with prophetic words. There are many stories of children filled with the Holy Spirit and used by God in powerful ways throughout history. For example, in revival camp meetings in the early 1800s, spontaneous child prophecy and preaching were common, leading many to repentance and conversion.[10] The same Holy Spirit that raised Jesus

---

[10]William L. De Arteaga, *Forging a Renewed Hebraic and Pauline Christianity*, 2011, MS., 183.

from the dead, the same Holy Spirit that has empowered us, will empower our children. They can prophesy, lay hands on the sick, and cast out demons.

When the Bible speaks about training up a child in the way they should go, it is not only speaking of good morals. The gifts and calling of the Lord are already theirs. It is our job to discover what they are and train them to walk in them. What is the direction of their destiny in Christ? This is the way they should go. What is the call on their life? This is the way they should go. What are the gifting and the empowerment of the Spirit in their life? This is the way they should go.

This is the training our children need from us to grow in the ways and the purposes of God for their lives. If we do this and give them our support to become who Jesus has called them to be, then, "When they are old they will not depart from it." Rather, they will fulfill the purposes for which they were created.

Today we are claiming our children for the kingdom of God, committing to nurture and train them in the things of the Spirit, and prophesying over their future, calling out their destinies, gifts, and callings to the praise and glory of God!

As for my daughters, they both prophesy and have received many dreams and visions over the years.

Prayer

> *Father God, You have given me these children to train up in the way they should go. You have created them for kingdom purpose, and they are never too young to praise You, prophesy, or walk by the Spirit. Teach me and lead me in the training of my children. Speak to me about their identities and destiny. Connect me with others who are training up their children in the things of the Spirit. Watch over and protect my children, stir up their gifts, fill them with Your Holy Spirit, and keep them walking in the way they should go all the days of their lives! In Jesus' name, Amen.*

Activation

Write down the names of all your children, grandchildren, nieces, nephews, and children who are not a part of your bloodline, but God has put them in your life in some way.

One by one, invite the Holy Spirit to speak to you about who they are in the kingdom. What Bible character would represent the type of gifting and calling on their life? What kind of talent, spiritual gift, and job does He have for them? Who are they called to influence?

Invite the Holy Spirit to give you a prophetic promise for each one, including a Scripture, a song, and anything else He gives you. Write it out into a prayer declaration to pray and declare regularly over their life.

Invite the Holy Spirit to speak to you about how to support and encourage them "in the way they should go," what kind of teaching and training they need, and how you can partner with God to see them receive it.

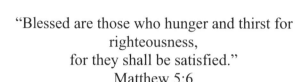

> "Blessed are those who hunger and thirst for
> righteousness,
> for they shall be satisfied."
> Matthew 5:6

I have five grandsons. They are growing up so fast. Over the last two years, as I have watched them getting older so quickly, I have been asking the Lord how to have an influence in their lives for the kingdom. He said, "Create hunger."

One evening, my husband and I were having dinner with them. My oldest grandson, Ian, was excited to show me he had gotten his first phone. It had limited capability, but because he and I both have iPhones we can text from anywhere in the world over Wi-Fi.

A light bulb went on. The Holy Spirit gave me a brilliant idea. Everywhere I go in the world, I take selfies and send them. Not just any selfie. Selfies with natural wonders, selfies with manmade wonders, selfie videos with the people I am ministering to. I tell him what I am doing and why, and ask people I am with to say hello using his name in their own language. I record videos of miracles, healings, and people who have been touched powerfully by the Lord. I send them to him from everywhere I am in the world.

He loves it. He asks me questions about what I do and what God is doing. He gets excited about the healings and miracles. He is dreaming of doing mission trips with me and seeing the world. It is creating hunger for the things of God.

Now, his younger brother just got his first phone. Guess what was the *first* thing he did? He asked Grandma to send him selfies and videos from all over the world.

Who in your life needs their hunger to be stirred? A child? A family member? A church? Stir their hunger and they will begin to seek God for His presence and kingdom. God will answer their hunger. Perhaps you are a grandparent and your children are far from the Lord and not leading your grandchildren in the ways of God. Parents often come to the Lord, or back to the Lord, when God gets a hold of their children!

Prayer

> *Father God, You have placed me in relationship with many people who don't know you, or don't long for more of You. Give me the kind of relationship with You that makes them jealous! Do signs, wonders, and miracles in and through my life to create testimonies of Jesus that will create great hunger for the things of God! Give me eyes to see myself as catalyst for creating hunger, and my relationships and everyday acquaintances as an opportunity for Your kingdom to come on earth as it is in heaven! In Jesus' name, Amen.*

Activation

Invite the Holy Spirit to show you who needs their hunger stirred. Write down their names. Now invite the Holy Spirit to give you creative ideas about how to stir up their hunger! Watch what happens!

DAY 84: BE HEALED!

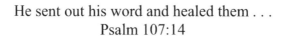

He sent out his word and healed them . . .
Psalm 107:14

". . . they will lay their hands on the sick and they will recover."
Mark 16:18

Jesus is the same yesterday, and today, and forever.
Hebrews 13:8

Sickness is not a test of patience or submission, and it does not glorify God. It is not sent by God to be endured as our "cross to bear." It is not God's will. God's will is to heal, deliver, and save people, while destroying all the works of the devil. Sin, sickness, and Satan are afflictions that oppress our minds, bodies, and souls. Jesus is a healer, and so are you.

The Bible is full of healing miracles. History is full of healing miracles. Our lives can be full of healing miracles too. Jesus is the same yesterday, today, and forever. He is still healing today. In one week in Brazil, I witnessed two thousand healings. Deaf ears and blind eyes were opened. Pain left, people got out of wheelchairs, and tumors disappeared.

It happens all over the world. I was in London. During worship, I felt a great heaviness on my chest. I could barely breathe. I said, "Lord, what is this?" I had an impression in my mind: "heart condition." It was a word of knowledge.

A word of knowledge is a supernatural knowing of facts or information we cannot discover through study or personal experience. It is one of the prophetic gifts of the Spirit. We can hear it by the voice of God to our hearts and mind. We can feel it physically or emotionally like I felt this heaviness in my chest. We can see it like a picture in our mind or like a vision. We can simply know it, like a thought that pops into our mind. We can read it like words written across a person's forehead.

I interrupted the worship and asked if anyone in the room had a heart condition because God wanted to heal them. A young man, twenty-six years old, came to the front. He was the only one in the room with a heart condition. I prayed for him. Nothing seemed to happen.

Three weeks later, I received a note from the pastor. The young man had been a visitor to the church that night. He had given up on life because he had an enlarged heart, could barely breathe, and was going to have open heart surgery. After that night and being prayed for, he went back to the doctor. Something was different. After testing the young man, the doctor said he was healed. His heart was completely normal. No surgery was needed. No more medical care was needed. It was a *miracle* of healing!

Jesus tells us, "Whenever you enter a town . . . heal the sick in it and say to them, 'The kingdom of God has come near to you'" (Luke 10:8-9).

Prayer

> *Father, I want to see miracles! I know it is Your will to heal. You tell us to heal the sick. You have given me the Holy Spirit and the power to heal. As I lay hands on the sick, Father, heal them. Give me boldness and a compassion for anyone who needs healing. Activate the gift of words of knowledge for healing in my life. In Jesus' name, Amen.*

Activation

Have you ever received a word of knowledge? Did you see it, read it, feel it, or think it? The gift of words of knowledge, like prophecy, is a gift of the Holy Spirit. You can ask for them! God heals with and without a word of knowledge, but words of knowledge help direct us. Having a word of knowledge about an illness, pain, or physical condition increases our faith to lay hands on a person for their healing. It increases the faith of the people we are praying for, knowing that God spoke to us about their condition. When God gives us a word of knowledge for healing, He intends to heal them!

☐ Invite the Holy Spirit to give you a word of knowledge about someone you will meet today. Just wait on Him for a few minutes. You may receive a slight impression—a thought that comes to mind. You may feel a pain or sensation in your body, or an emotion. You may see a picture or words in your mind.

- ☐ Ask Him to show you a face, a name, or some other way to identify who needs healing.
- ☐ Write it all down.

When you meet the person today, step out in faith and release healing to them.

DAY 85: THERE IS POWER IN THE NAME OF JESUS

"Whatever you ask in my name, this I will do,
that the Father may be glorified in the Son.
If you ask me anything in my name, I will do it."
John 14:13-14

And Jesus came and said to them, "All authority
in heaven and on earth has been given to me. Go
therefore and make disciples of all nations,
baptizing them in the name of the Father and of
the Son and of the Holy Spirit, teaching them to
observe all that I have commanded you. And
behold, I am with you always,
to the end of the age."
Matthew 28:18-20

God is up to something big in the world. We are living in a time of deliverance and breakthrough in the midst of violent change. We are about to witness a demonstration of the gospel in this generation no generation has ever seen. What is this move of God? It is a move of the Holy Spirit with healing, miracles, signs, and wonders. It is the reclaiming of the power of the name of Jesus Christ.

There is power in the name of Jesus. It shakes the kingdom of darkness, awakens angels to His purposes, shifts atmospheres, and releases God's will on the earth. Everything—every problem, circumstance, demon, and, one day, every knee—must bow to the name of Jesus.

Not just to any god, to Jesus. Jesus is Savior, Lord, Protector, Deliverer, Healer, God Almighty, the Anointed One, the Bright and Morning Star, the Alpha and the Omega, the one and only Son of the Living God. He is Mighty God, Everlasting Father, King of Kings, Lord of Lords, and Wonderful Counselor. The Light of the World, Prince of Peace, the Lamb who takes away the sin of the world, the Lion of the Tribe of Judah.

And He is Immanuel—God with us!

His name is more excellent than any angel. He is the begotten Son of God seated at the right hand of majesty! His name is above every other name! His name conquers the power of sin, disease, death, and hell!

We are in Him and He is in us. His power is with us because the Holy Spirit has been poured out on us. His authority is ours through this relationship by faith in His name. We are born into the family of God—co-heirs with Christ. We are baptized into the name of Jesus and into Christ Himself. We are commissioned as ambassadors to go in His name to the nations.

We have the *right* to use His name and exercise His authority against our enemies (Ephesians 6:12), in our petitions (John 14:13-14), in our worship (Revelations 15:3-4), and in our mission (Mark 16:15-18).

Prayer

> *Jesus, Your name is wonderful, powerful, and beautiful. Thank You for giving us Your name, the name above all names, the name that heals, casts out demons, and destroys the works of darkness. It is the name by which we are saved, healed, delivered, and answered. I will ask for miracles in Your great and powerful name, right now, today, and every day for the rest of my life. I know I have what I ask for in Your name. Thank You for giving us Your name. Thank You, thank You, thank You. In Your name, Jesus, Amen.*

Activation

This is a time to worship Jesus. It is time to reclaim the power of His name. Invite the Holy Spirit to bring this truth alive in you as you sing.

Can you hear the battle cry?

Here is the song I'm singing over you right now. I invite you to sing it over your family, your city, your nation.

"Break Every Chain" by Will Reagan

There is power, in the name of Jesus.
There is power in the name of Jesus.
There is power, in the name of Jesus
To break every chain, break every chain break every chain.

All sufficient sacrifice
So freely given, such a price
For our redemption
heaven's gates swing wide.

There's an army rising up
There's an army rising up
There's an army rising up
To break every chain break, break every chain, break every chain.[11]

DAY 86: FOR THE SAKE OF THE WORLD

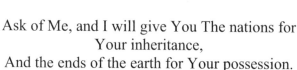

Ask of Me, and I will give You The nations for
Your inheritance,
And the ends of the earth for Your possession.
Psalm 2:8 NKJV

How beautiful upon the mountains are the feet
of him who brings good news, who publishes
peace, who brings good news of happiness,
who publishes salvation . . .
Isaiah 52:7

Therefore prophesy concerning the land of
Israel, and say to the mountains and hills, to the
ravines and valleys, Thus says the Lord God
". . . you shall shoot forth your branches and
yield your fruit to my people Israel, for they
will soon come home. For behold, I am for
you, and I will turn to you, and you shall be
tilled and sown. And I will multiply people on
you, the whole house of Israel, all of it. The
cities shall be inhabited and the waste places
rebuilt. And I will multiply on you man and
beast, and they shall multiply and be fruitful.
And I will cause you to be inhabited as in your
former times, and will do more good to you
than ever before. Then you will know that I am
the Lord."
Ezekiel 36:4-11

I was sitting in the back of the church. I had come to the meeting because I
heard the prophet Cindy Jacobs was coming to release a prophetic word
over California, the state where I live. The Lord had put a love and a concern
in my heart for my state, city, and country.

Soon after worship ended, Cindy walked up to the platform and said, "Kim, I have a word for you!" I nearly fell out of my seat! She asked me to come to the front and when I did, she started to yell, "The Lord says, 'Ask me for the nations' and I will give them, and I will give you great favor . . .'"

Something hit me right in my guts. When I got home, I was still shaking, but I got on my knees and asked the Lord for the nations.

The nations are on the heart of God. Political figures and governments are all fighting for control of various spheres of authority, but the government of the nations belongs to Jesus. The problems, corruption, poverty, diseases, and natural disasters all find their answers, solutions, and healing in Christ.

God's people—you and I—have the answers, solutions, and healing within us for the nations. We carry the kingdom of God. We can receive the prophetic word of the Lord to declare over lands and see it respond. We can receive the prophetic word of the Lord for solutions to problems and answers to questions. Jesus spoke to a fig tree and it withered. Ezekiel spoke to dry bones and an army was raised. Joseph interpreted a dream and solved the problem of famine.

We have good news for the nations. The nations belong to Jesus. They are His inheritance. We are co-heirs with Christ—therefore, the nations belong to us, too.

I prophesy over you today, "The Lord would say to you, 'Ask me for the nations and I will give them to you. I will give you great favor and open doors. I will release to you prophetic words for their future, and for their present, solutions to problems and answers to questions. I will put a sword in your mouth to cut off the enemy from the land and a sickle in your hand to bring in my harvest, says the Lord. Ask me for the nations and I will give them to you."

Prayer

> *Father, I ask You for the nations. I ask You to give me Your heart, Your word, and Your desire for the nations. Send me and I will go. Put Your word in my mouth and I will speak. Give me*

a burden and I will pray. Give me the nations as an inheritance. In Jesus' name, Amen.

Activation

Invite the Holy Spirit to put the name of a nation (or nations) on your heart. Ask Him what His heart is for the nation and its people. Ask Him what the hardships and needs of the people are.

Consider doing further research about its history and its problems. Make a prayer list. Pray for the nation. Practice prophesying over the nation, its land, people, government, and problems by writing in a journal. Use Scripture and the words God gives you.

Invite the Holy Spirit to do the same in you for your own country.

DAY 87: HISTORY MAKERS

At strategic times in history, God has chosen
women and empowered them with His Holy
Spirit to carry out His will in extraordinary
ways. He chose Mary to give birth to the Savior.
He chose another Mary to be the first apostle to
proclaim the good news of His resurrection.
And He chose women in the early church to
pastor, teach, and proclaim the gospel. Women
were coworkers with the apostle Paul and joint
heirs together with Christ and their brothers in
the faith. And at the dawn of the greatest revival
since the day of Pentecost, He bestowed on a
humble woman—Agnes Ozman—the privilege
and responsibility of being the first to
experience and proclaim the Pentecostal
baptism of the Spirit in the 20th century.
Throughout the century, He called countless
women and empowered them to fulfill both
humble and high-profile assignments. In the 20th
century, Spirit-filled women began to discover
that these women were not exceptions to God's
plan, but instead were His prototypes for God's
woman.
Susan C. Hyatt[12]

Throughout history there have been brave Christian women who have
impacted and influenced society. They led movements and impacted
generations even when the culture into which they were born limited women
in ministry. Proverbs says our gift makes room for us.

---

[12]Susan C. Hyatt, "Spirit-Filled Women," Vinson Synan, *The Century of the Holy Spirit: 100
Years of Pentecostal and Charismatic Renewal 1901-2001,* (Nashville, TN: Thomas Nelson,
2001), 262.

- In the 1400s, Joan of Arc in France was visited by the voice of God through angelic messengers. At sixteen, she dared to request to lead the armies of the nation in order to restore the throne to the rightful king of France and free the nation from the grip of England. She succeeded in her quest.
- In the 1500s, St. Teresa of Avila, a Carmelite nun and mystic, wrote the famous book *The Interior Castle*, which has guided millions of people into the presence of God.
- In the 1600s, Susanna Wesley was responsible for the teaching and mentoring of her two revivalist sons, John and Charles Wesley.
- In the 1800s, Harriet Tubman formed the Philadelphia Female Anti-Slavery Society. She was a Christian who escaped slavery and went on to lead an influential movement within the Underground Railroad saving hundreds of slaves. Also, Florence Nightingale, a social reformer and founder of modern-day nursing fought to improve healthcare for wounded soldiers and affected healthcare for all.
- In the 19th century, Phoebe Palmer was a major leader in the Holiness movement. She played a significant role in spreading the concept of Christian holiness throughout the world. In her book, *The Promise of the Father*, Palmer defended the idea of women in Christian ministry. Also, Francis Willard led two million members in the temperance movement to protect society from alcoholism, helped pass child labor laws, and started kindergartens and daycare for working families.
- In the 20th century, the missionary movement was led by women, sending 856 single women missionaries into the world and translating the Bible for hundreds of language groups. Carrie Judd Montgomery and Mariah Woodsworth-Etter were known around the world as leaders in the healing movement. Aimee Semple McPherson became the most recognized and prominent woman leader of the Pentecostal movement and the founder of the International Church of the Foursquare Gospel.
- Who can forget Kathryn Kuhlman? She was one of the most well-known healing evangelists in history.

These are only a few examples of the women throughout history who dared to answer the call of God on their lives. They believed in something greater than themselves. They believed that the gospel could change the world. Their hearts burned with passion for the lost, the broken, the sick, the poor, the widow, and the orphan. They looked at society and the culture of their day and lifted up their voice, offered their hands and feet, and laid down their lives to create something better, something holier, something pleasing to the heart of God.

Women change the world when they rise up and lead.

Prayer

> *Father, our world, nation, cities, and families need us to rise up and receive a vision for what can be. We need to believe again that we can be a part of a movement that makes history and impacts generations to come. We need healers, prophets, missionaries, and governmental leaders from our ranks to lead armies of women to battle against the dark forces in our societies and cultures. We hear the testimony of the stories from women in the past. We hear the cry of the oppressed and needy. Break our hearts for the lost. Fill us with passion for the broken. Give us the Spirit in greater measure and give us a voice to carry Your message of revival in our lands! In Jesus' name, Amen!*

Activation

Who are the great women leaders God raised up in your nation? What is their story? How did they impact the nation? How does this impact you?

DAY 88: SEND ME!

And he said to them, "Go into all the world and
proclaim the gospel to the whole creation.
Whoever believes and is baptized will be saved,
but whoever does not believe will be
condemned. And these signs will accompany
those who believe: in my name they will cast
out demons; they will speak in new tongues;
they will pick up serpents with their hands; and
if they drink any deadly poison, it will not hurt
them; they will lay their hands on the sick, and
they will recover."
Mark 16:15-18

We were born to live supernatural lives. We were born to be a part of something far bigger than our own lives. We were born to raise the dead, heal the sick, and send demons fleeing. We were born to be sent into the world with a word of the Lord in our mouth and the love of Christ in our heart. We were born to make history. We are the sent ones.

Jesus came, died, and rose again so that we could be made whole, reconciled to God, and ready to receive power. He poured out His Spirit so that we could be empowered for the mission. He gave us His name so we would have authority over the kingdom of darkness.

If God is for us, who can be against us? No one. God is with us to bear witness to His Word through signs and wonders and miracles. Jesus has gone ahead of us. He has conquered sin and death. He has made a way for us to be more than conquerors.

We are miracle workers. We are supernatural superwomen. All of us are Wonder Woman.

And we are being sent into the world to proclaim the gospel to all creation.

Come on! Let's *go!*

Prayer

> *Father, You have done it all. You have already won the victory through the life, death, and resurrection of Your Son, my Savior and Lord, Jesus Christ! You have called, anointed, and appointed me to step into the victory of Jesus. You have clothed me with power from on high and seated me in heavenly places with Christ. You have armed me with the name of Jesus, empowered me with the same Spirit that raised Christ from the dead, and given me the gift of eternal life. I am sent out into the world to bring the message of the kingdom everywhere I go to everyone I meet, and You will be with me to perform miracles. My life is more than I once thought. I am Yours, Lord. You are mine. We cannot lose! Today, Father, I accept the call on my life. Today, Father, as I step out of my front door, I go as one sent by You—called, anointed, and appointed. I will lay hands on the sick, cast out demons, prophesy, and love all those who cross my path. I will see my home, family, workplace, co-workers, neighborhood, city, and nation as my mission field! In Jesus' name, Amen!*

Activation

Take the devotion above and rewrite it. Replace every "we" or "us" with "I" and "me" so that it becomes a personal declaration about your identity and purpose. Read it out loud. Shout it into the air. Believe it!

Invite the Holy Spirit to show you your mission field. It will be all the places where you already are right now and will include all the people that come into your life or across your path.

Write them down. Have you understood this was your assignment and mission field in this season? How does seeing the places and people in your life as a mission field change your thinking and actions toward them? Invite the Holy Spirit to give you vision for what the Lord desires to do through you for these places and people.

Invite the Holy Spirit to help you envision the world. Ask Him to show you what nation He is sending you to. Ask Him to show you what He has for you to do there. Ask Him to give you a plan and provision for this vision.

Watch what He will do!

DAY 89: DIS-ABLED NO MORE!

"And ought not this woman,
a daughter of Abraham
whom Satan bound for
eighteen years,
be loosed from this bond
on the Sabbath day?"
Luke 13:16

And he laid his hands on her,
and immediately she was made straight,
and she glorified God.
Luke 13:13

This is a prophetic picture of a woman delivered from all that has disabled her. This disability was not caused by sin. It was not caused by illness. It was a bondage, an enslavement, an imprisonment, and an assignment from the pit of hell set against her from the time she was created to keep her from her destiny.

Women are created in the image of God to bring Him glory! From the beginning, it has been the scheme of the enemy to keep us from becoming who we really are and bringing glory to God!

In this story, we find a religious spirit that objects to the woman being set free. A religious spirit will always question our freedom and offer to keep us limited and dis-empowered. But Jesus answers with our rightful place and identity. We are daughters of Abraham, and the daughters of Abraham are free women of God.

The most beautiful part of this is the result of her freedom—His adversaries are put to shame and the people rejoice over the miraculous works of God.

We are the daughters of Abraham! We are the free women of faith. Let us be loosed from any religious spirit that seeks to limit, shame, and dis-empower us. Let us be free to bring glory to God by the freedom we have in Christ Jesus to say and do the wonderful works of God. Let us be filled with and empowered by the Holy Spirit and continue the mission of Christ to the world.

This is what Jesus is doing among women in this hour. *Why?* Adam was made in the image of God. In His image, God made Adam—male and female. Male and female together are the image of God. Therefore, the face of God, His image on the earth, cannot be fully revealed in the kingdom without us!

I hear the Lord say, "I have brought you here. It is my doing, and it is good. I have a work in you to do, for I have a work for you to do. I have a call for you to answer. I have a woman's work in the kingdom that can no longer be delayed. It is time. It is time that the ones called woman become who I have created them to be. I am loosing womanhood. I am loosing women. I am loosing the daughters of Abraham from every adversarial spirit that has disabled them. The devil is no match for them as they walk the earth—as they receive the empowerment that I have ordained for them from the beginning. I am breathing over them. I am laboring over them. I am brooding over them and speaking my word. Woman, you are freed from your dis-ability. I make you able. I make you free. I have made you woman."

Prayer

> *Father God, I am Your woman! I am here to glorify You and bring You glory! I am a daughter of Abraham, a free woman of faith! You are for me—therefore, who can be against me? Thank You for the gift of freedom without shame. In Jesus' name, Amen.*

Activation

Invite the Holy Spirit to reveal to you anywhere you feel you have been limited or disabled in the call on your life due to a religious spirit or false belief. Invite Him to set you free and reveal to you the truth about your freedom in Christ.

243

For further research, here is my favorite article on women in the service of the church by N.T. Wright: http://ntwrightpage.com/2016/07/12/womens-service-in-the-church-the-biblical-basis/

BE FREE!

DAY 90: *TALITHA CUMI!*

"Why are you making a commotion and
weeping? The child is not dead but sleeping."
And they laughed at him. But he put them all
outside and took the child's father and mother
and those who were with him and went in where
the child was. Taking her by the hand he said to
her, "*Talitha cumi*," which means,
"Little girl, I say to you, arise."
Mark 5:39-41

Arise, my love, my beautiful one, and come
away, for behold, the winter is past; the rain is
over and gone. The flowers appear on the earth,
the time of singing has come, and the voice of
the turtledove is heard in our land . . .
Arise, my love, my beautiful one, and come
away . . . let me see your face, let me hear
your voice, for your voice is sweet,
and your face is lovely.
Song of Songs 2:10-14

I was standing in front of a group of women when I spotted her. She was crouched in her seat, looking down, her arms hugging her own waist. I heard, "*Talitha cumi*." Then the Lord said, "She feels dead inside, but she is only sleeping. Today is a new day. It will be a fresh awakening. She has a destiny. She has gifts. She is my beloved. I will awaken her and she will arise. *Talitha cumi!*"

What needs awakening in your life? Who do you know that needs awakening? *Talitha cumi!*

When the winter is over, new life arises and intimate love blooms. Our confidence is restored, we are seen for who we really are, and our voice is lifted for all to hear. Jesus is calling us to arise and receive a fresh outpouring of His love and grace. Jesus is calling us to arise and fulfill the purposes for which we were created. In order to arise, we must first be awakened! Too many of us, and the women we know, feel dead inside because of the harshness or difficulties of their childhood or perhaps the boredom of day-to-day life.

Talitha cumi!

Sometimes we feel dead inside and have fallen asleep because of the company we have been keeping. Sometimes it's our religious rituals that make a commotion but are empty of the life of the Spirit. Sometimes it is the distractions.

Notice, when Jesus goes to awaken the little girl, there are those around her making a commotion and weeping over her death. They don't see any future for her. They don't see beyond the moment. They don't see the awakening that is coming. They don't see her with the eyes of Jesus. Jesus puts them outside. He closes the door on their unbelief. He closes the door on the distraction they bring. He closes the door on their blindness.

And He takes her by the hand. *Talitha cumi!*

Prayer

> *Father, take me by the hand and awaken me! Clear away the distractions, close the door on unbelief and blindness whether it is in me or those around me. Raise me from the dead on the inside so that I may arise! In Jesus' name, Amen.*

Activation

Make a list of the women you know who need to be awakened in order that they may arise! Include your name in the list.

Call each of them by name one at a time and shout, *"Talitha cumi!* Awaken and arise!"* (Tah-Leetha-koo-me)

MORE BOOKLETS BY DR. KIM MAAS

PROPHECY AND PROPHETIC
COMMUNITY SERIES

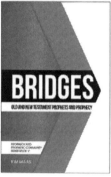

Dr. Kim Maas has a powerful new 6 booklet series, Prophecy and Prophetic Community. Each booklet unpacks an aspect of the prophetic and prophetic community in the local church. Whether you are new to the prophetic and wanting to learn more, or are established in the prophetic and want to go deeper – this series has something for everyone.

Booklet 1: The Power of Words - Can We Be Trusted With God's Secrets?
Booklet 2: Foundations - What the Bible Says About Prophecy
Booklet 3: The Gift of Prophecy - Part 1
Booklet 4: The Gift of Prophecy - Part 2
Booklet 5: Bridges - Old and New Testament Prophets and Prophecy
Booklet 6: Prophecy Q&A.

Available on-line through Ten35Productions @ www.kimmmaas.com

FACING ZIKLAG:
TURNING CRISIS INTO CROWNS

Crisis comes to everyone. It is a strategy devised by the enemy to keep you from your God-given destiny and often comes moments before the fulfilment of a prophetic promise. No one is immune. David was only twelve days from becoming king and receiving the crown prophesied to him by Samuel when he faced the events at Ziklag. The enemy hit him hard in a place and in a way he did not expect or anticipate, turning his world upside down. His decisions would be crucial to the outcome.

In this two-part booklet, you will discover how David's choices and response to God during the most pivotal moment in his life make all the difference in turning his crisis in to a crown. Gain the insight, keys, and strategy you need for facing, navigating, and overcoming your own Ziklag moments, with unwavering faith and courage.

The Facing Ziklag Companion Journal is a "must have" to help you work through your own Ziklag moment and move you forward to see your crisis turned into a crown.

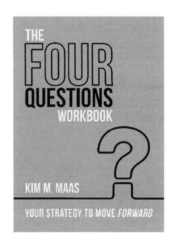

ABOUT DR. KIM MAAS

Dr. Kim Maas is an international speaker and the Founder of Kim Maas Ministries, Inc. She has trained and equipped churches, ministries, and individuals to operate in the gift of prophecy in several nations and the United States. After a radical encounter with the Holy Spirit March 22, 1994, Kim left her twenty-two year nursing career to serve God full time. Her passion is to inspire, encourage and equip God's people to move forward toward fulfilling the call of God on their lives. This passion comes through in her preaching, leadership, writing, and everyday life. She is the president and C.E.O. of KIM MAAS MINISTRIES, Inc. and the founder and director of Women of Our Time (WOOT). In addition to speaking, preaching, and writing, she served as a pastor in the local church for over 12 years before becoming a full time itinerant minister. Kim earned a Doctorate in Ministry at United Theological Seminary and a Master of Divinity at King's University. Kim and her husband Mike live in Moorpark, CA. They have three grown children and five grandchildren.

For more information about Dr. Kim Maas or to invite her to speak at your next event visit: kimmaas.com

To follow her on twitter: @pkmaas
Or, write Kim at: hello@kimmaas.com

Dr. Kim Maas
P.O. Box 271
Moorpark, CA 93020

Made in the USA
Middletown, DE
02 April 2021